Environmental Activities

Susan Godfrey

Bright Ideas
for Early Years

Published by Scholastic Publications Ltd,
Villiers House, Clarendon Avenue,
Leamington Spa, Warwickshire
CV32 5PR

© 1992 Scholastic Publications

Written by Susan Godfrey
Edited by Janet Fisher
Sub-edited by Christine Lee
and Jo Saxelby
Illustrations by Ursula Sieger
Cover design by Anna Oliwa
Cover photograph by Martyn Chillmaid
Photographs by Bob Bray (pages 21 and
31), John Twinning (page 5), and John
Walmsley (page 77)

Every attempt has been made to trace
and acknowledge the photographers
whose pictures appear in this book. The
publishers apologise for any omissions.

Artwork by David Harban Design,
Warwick
Printed in Great Britain by
Loxley Brothers Ltd, Sheffield

British Library Cataloguing in Publication Data
A catalogue record of this book is available from the British
Library.

ISBN 0-590-53024-0

**To Gail, my colleague, in
appreciation of her constant
interest and enthusiasm.**

Contents

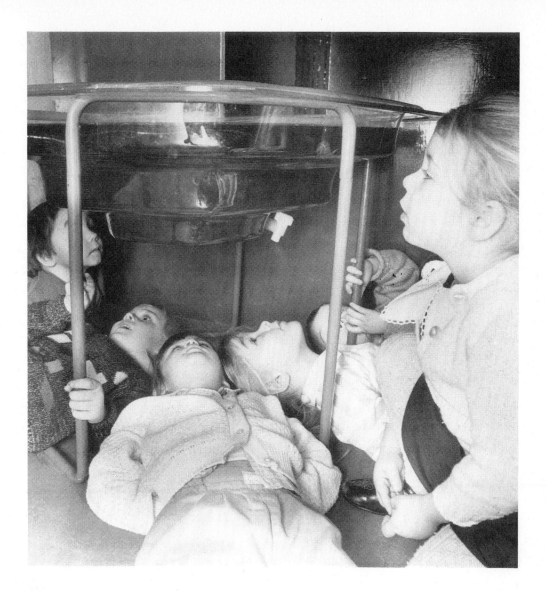

Introduction

From an early age, children have a natural curiosity about the people, places, animals, plants and materials around them. They learn about their environment through their own first-hand experience, from their parents, through the media and from a variety of other sources. Schools have a vital role to play in helping their pupils make sense of these experiences and in developing their knowledge and understanding of the physical and human processes which interact to shape the environment.

The natural resources that are readily accessible will obviously vary immensely according to location, depending upon whether you are close to the sea, the mountains, the countryside or the city. It is not always possible to take very young children on trips to explore different types of environment, but you can make considerable use of your immediate surroundings, the children's own experiences of expeditions with family and friends and your own travels.

The man-made environment must, of course, be explored alongside the natural world. Houses, shops, boats, bridges and roads can all be explored and discussed. Why a bridge? Why this sort of bridge? Why a boat? Which building is the tallest?

Schools can also help to foster a reasoned and sensitive concern for the management of the earth's resources. Several of the activities in the book are aimed at increasing awareness of the importance of conservation. Encouraging saving, reusing and recycling must be emphasised. With so much packaging, disposable material, numerous plastic bags and tins it is difficult for children to grasp that there is a real need for control in this area and these are, of course, matters of increasing social concern.

Environmental education has four overlapping elements:
● curiosity and awareness about the environment;
● knowledge and understanding;
● skills;
● informed concern.

By becoming a collector yourself, and encouraging the children to do likewise, you will soon build up a collection of natural and man-made materials — stones, shells, bark, feathers, cones, seeds and items of household waste such as cartons and boxes — for the children's own investigations. Encourage free play with as many as possible. Ask the children to help tidy and clear up afterwards — a learning situation which will help to develop a responsible and caring attitude towards their surroundings. Growing indoors or in the outside play area need not be confined to a few cress seeds or the odd marigold — provide large containers, beg or borrow plants, seed potatoes, bulbs and corms and encourage a flamboyant display throughout the year.

Many of the activities can also be enhanced by parental involvement. If parents and other members of the family can be encouraged to take an interest in and support children at this early stage, the link will be an invaluable help to the child's education.

The work undertaken in school should enable younger children to *begin* to:

• gain, at first hand, knowledge of their local environment, for example, its weather, surface features and human influences, such as buildings, roads and so on;

• gain knowledge of the use of materials and energy in their environment;

• compare the main features of their local environment with others they have visited and, as far as possible, with more distant places;

• relate the present to the past environment;

• gain some understanding of the life cycle of animals and plants;

• apply to environmental matters their developing skills in making careful observations, predicting consequences, asking questions, using a variety of sources of information and interpreting the information gained, and communicating their findings in a variety of ways;

• develop an understanding of the interdependence of people and their environment;

• develop a commitment to the informed care and improvement of their environment and that of others.

It is with these thoughts in mind, which have been taken and adapted from *Environmental Education* (HMSO), that the activities in this book have been developed. Their aim is not only to increase children's general awareness but also to provide ideas that will encourage a young child to investigate his own environment and to stimulate questioning and imaginative thinking.

7

Items to collect

Many of the items necessary for the activities in this book will already be in use in the busy early years classroom. The list below offers suggestions for further items you may wish to collect.

Articles with interesting textures
Balls of wool
Binoculars
Bolts
Buckets
Cameras (old)
Cardboard boxes (large)
Cleaning equipment
Clock
Clothes (old)
Dolls' house furniture
Empty bottles
Fish tank
Flower pots
Gym mats or carpet scraps
Herbs
Hosepipe
House bricks (few)
Kaleidoscope
Keys (old)
Lantern

Locks
Magazines
Magnets
Magnifying glasses
Mini microscopes
Mirrors
Night-light
Paddling pool
Pegs
Percussion instruments
Pot pourri
Radio (small)
Shakers
Shoes
Spices
Tape recorder
Telephone (a toy or an old one)
Templates – farm animals, vehicles
Toothbrushes (old)
Torch
Toy cars, lorries and buildings
Transparent bin liners
Trays (shallow)
Video recorder
Wallpaper book
Washing line
Washing-up equipment

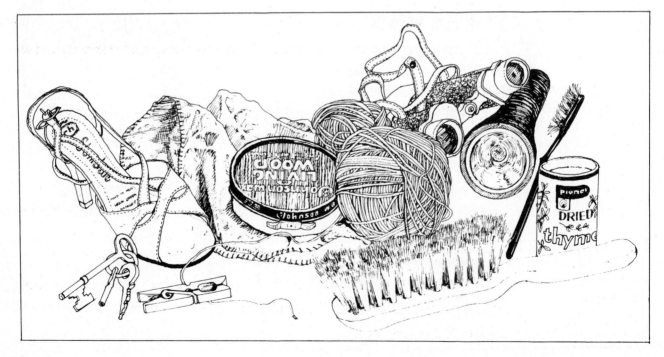

Ourselves, family and friends

Chapter 1

Activities which help to develop self-awareness are the ideal starting point for environmental studies. By encouraging children to observe themselves, we can help them establish their own self-image and their place in relation to family, friends and adults, such as teachers, who are part of their daily lives. Further skills of observation and communication will contribute to a greater understanding, not only of their immediate surroundings, but of the world outside the home and school. The activities in this chapter could become starting points for projects.

Our photographs

Objective

To increase self-awareness and encourage an understanding of the relationship between home and school.

What you need

Sheets of paper, adhesive sticks, felt-tipped pens, crayons.

What to do

Make envelopes, either by pre-folding the paper for younger children or encouraging older ones to measure and fold the paper themselves, as in Figure 1. Secure the edges with adhesive. Let the children decorate their envelopes with either simple drawings or their names.

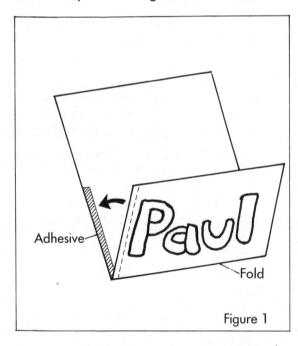

Figure 1

Ask the children to take the envelope home and, if possible, to enclose a photograph of themselves and bring it back to school. Mount the photographs, adding the child's name in clear letters underneath.

Follow-up

• Collect some old cameras for the children to play with. Use old photographs to make an album. Pictures of weddings, holidays, cars and places will all spark off discussions.
• Make a photograph album of people that help us. Include your own photographs of teachers, caretakers, cooks and so on.

Questions

Who is that? Is that his mummy? Is that your house? Can you see your garden? Were you a baby then?

Faces

Objective

To encourage close scrutiny of faces and increase awareness of self-image.

What you need

Mirrors, copies of photocopiable page 83.

What to do

Allow the children free use of the mirrors, discussing with them the main features of their faces. Talk about the face chart on photocopiable page 83. What do the faces convey? Play a game. Point to a face and see if the children can imitate that expression. Is the expression happy, sad, surprised etc?

Follow-up

● Ask the children to paint simple faces, encouraging them to remember all the main features. Alternatively, let them work with collage on a pre-cut 'head' shape to create a face.
● Encourage the children to search through magazines and cut out faces to make a book. Talk about expressions, ages etc.
● Take photographs at special moments and mount them in a book.

Questions

What makes you happy? Can you remember anything that makes you sad? How do you feel when you are angry? In what ways are we the same? How do we differ?

My body can

Objective

To develop a feeling and awareness for specific body movements.

What you need

A selection of percussion instruments, paper, pencils, crayons etc.

What to do

Talk with the children about main body movements, encouraging them to suggest some themselves. Encourage the children to try the movements. Use percussion instruments to provide the type of rhythm needed for the movements.

Teach the following rhyme to the children and get them to make the appropriate movements:

I can run,
I can jump,
I can twist,
I can skip,
I can hop up and down
Or quietly sit.
I can walk,
I can stand,
I can play all day,
I can bow to the Queen
Or run away.
(Susan Godfrey)

The acting of this rhyme is more successful with a small group. Take turns for each group to do the movements while the others say the rhyme.

Follow-up

• Let the children paint or draw pictures to depict certain movements. Alternatively, ask them to find pictures of dancers, skaters, footballers, and so on to compile a 'movement' book.

Questions

How do babies move? When can a baby walk? Why do old people move slowly?

My hands can

Objective

To encourage close observation and awareness of hands and how we use them.

What you need

Paper, pencils, scissors, adhesive, coloured sugar paper, magazines, a selection of items which involve different ways of using hands (such as modelling clay, scissors, cups and saucers, pencils, bricks, a xylophone).

What to do

Ask the children to draw around their hands — they may need help with this. Invite them to colour and cut out the shapes and let them mount them on coloured sugar paper. Encourage them to add their names. Let the children investigate the activities you have set out and encourage them to talk about the ways in which they are using their hands.

Follow-up

• Let the children take turns to talk about ways in which they have used their hands during the activity time. Ask the children to search through magazines for pictures of hands. Let them cut out and mount them, showing as many different uses as possible. Give the children some paper to take home to draw around mummy's, daddy's or baby's hand.
• Teach the children the rhyme 'Ten Little Soldiers' (*This Little Puffin*).

Questions

Whose hand is the largest? Which finger is longest? What does mummy do with her hands? What can you do with one hand?

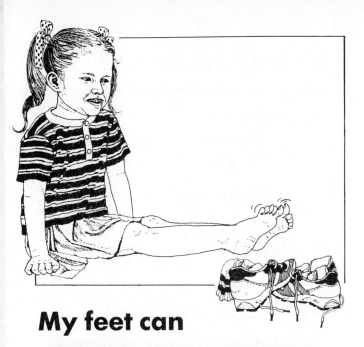

My feet can

Objective

To promote and encourage observation and awareness of feet and how we use them.

What you need

Tambourine, gym mats or rubber-backed underlay, shallow trays of water, large sheets of absorbent paper.

What to do

Ask the children to sit down in a circle, with their feet towards the centre. Tell them to take off their footwear and stretch out their feet. Encourage them to move their feet, keeping their legs as still as possible. Let them experiment and see how many movements they can achieve. Point out the heel, ankle and toes. Get the children to practise wiggling their toes in time to the shaking of a tambourine.

Now ask them to stand up and play 'Stepping over the stepping stones' (*This Little Puffin*), using individual rubber mats spaced out across the area. If you do not have gym mats, rubber-backed underlay makes a good alternative, cut to size and placed rubber side down.

While the children are barefooted, ask them to walk through the water trays and on to the paper. Compare their footprints. Encourage them to make further prints, using the whole foot, toes or heels.

Follow-up

- Let the children each make a footprint with paint to mount and keep. Encourage them to compare sizes.
- Ask the children to look for other footprints. Can they guess who made them? Was it an animal?
- Invite the children to draw around their shoes and cut out the shapes. Encourage them to measure with the shoe shape. How many shoe shapes are needed to cross the room? The playground?

Questions

Do you know what size shoe you take? Why do we wear shoes? Which activities are better done in bare feet?

A theme table

Objective

To identify and distinguish between the senses.

What you need

A large table covered with a cloth, collections of objects which involve the use of one of the five senses (for example, percussion instruments, a small radio and a ticking clock for hearing; articles with different textures for feeling; spices, herbs, flowers, pot pourri etc, for smelling; magnifying glasses, mirrors, a kaleidoscope, old binoculars, a camera, pictures, books and photograph albums for seeing; bowls of sugar, salt, lemon juice, tiny pieces of vegetables, fruit and cheese for tasting).

What to do
Each day for a week, display items connected with one of the five senses. Allow the children to observe and freely experiment with the articles each day. (Before the 'tasting' day, make sure that none of the children suffer from food allergies.)

Follow-up
• Make a set of 'sense' books using the children's own drawings or pictures cut from magazines.
• Make a feely book using different textured papers, fabric etc.
• Make a tape of familiar sounds and get the children to listen to it. Can they identify the sounds?

Questions
Can you find something that feels soft? Can you see with one eye? Which is your favourite smell, sound etc?

What can you feel?

Objective
To encourage sensitivity.

What you need
An outdoor area.

What to do
Take a walk with the children stopping to 'feel' at regular intervals — not only with hands but with feet and bodies. Encourage the children to touch and feel surfaces, plants, flowers and trees. Talk about the feel of the wind, the sun, raindrops or even snowflakes! Suggest that the children try touching objects with their eyes closed.

Follow-up
• Discuss the walk and encourage the children to talk about and try to describe the things they felt during their time outside.
• Take a feely walk inside!

Questions
Did the wind feel warm or cold? Which things felt hard, soft, rough, smooth? What could you feel with your feet?

Tracing the smell

Objective
To encourage an awareness of the sense of smell and to have fun!

What you need
A day when something particularly good is cooking in the school kitchen or another classroom, or painters are at work or a new playground surface is being laid.

What to do
Starting from the classroom, take the children for a short walk. Stop every so often and encourage the children to sniff the air. Make a note of any comments. Continue the walk, perhaps tracing the source of a particular smell. Perhaps you could all enjoy a freshly cooked cake from the oven or chat with the workmen before returning to the classroom.

Follow-up
* Talk about favourite smells, good smells and bad smells.
* Make a collection of items that smell interesting.

Questions
What could you smell outside? What did the smells tell you? Can you describe a smell that you like or dislike?

Who's talking?

Objective
To encourage the children to speak and listen and to introduce the concept of communication.

What you need
An old telephone or toy telephone, a small table, pen, paper or card.

What to do
Write a clear list of the children's names and telephone numbers on a large sheet of paper. (If some children do not have a telephone, let them make up a number.)

Arrange the telephone on a small table with the list nearby. Choose one child to hide his eyes or to sit with his back to the table. Choose another child to dial his number and say, for example, 'Hello Ben'. Ask the first child to try to identify the voice and then let him have a turn at dialling and speaking.

This is a very popular game which encourages the children to speak clearly and concentrate on listening carefully. Number recognition and the learning of individual telephone numbers add to the value of this activity.

Follow-up

• Allow the children to play freely and practise ringing their own telephone numbers.
• Talk about the use of the telephone — to give messages, orders or to call the emergency services. Stress the importance of the telephone's proper use and care. Extend the activity by using a box of cards with names, telephone numbers and addresses arranged in alphabetical order. This encourages the children to read and remember their number and address, and introduces them to an alphabetical system.
• Two telephones encourage conversation and could perhaps be used in a 'hospital corner' or a 'hairdressing salon'.

Questions

How else can we communicate with people? Which is the quickest method of communication?

What do we wear?

Objective

To encourage observation of clothing and uses of different types of material.

What you need

A box of carefully selected, clean, old clothes (such as jumpers, dresses, wool socks, cotton socks, swimsuits, mackintoshes etc), copies of photocopiable page 84, pencils, adhesive, thin card, paper, scissors, crayons, cardboard tubes.

What to do

Let the children take turns to pick an item out of the clothes box. Encourage them to talk about the garment they find. Is it worn on a cold day or a warm day? Is it adult size or child size? Is it for a baby? Is it for a special occasion? Arrange the clothes in sets as the game progresses.

Follow this with the card doll activity. Distribute copies of photocopiable page 84 and ask the children to stick them on to thin card then cut out the basic outline of the body shape. Let the children draw the facial features and colour in the vest and pants. Help them to draw around the shape to make paper 'clothes' with tabs

which can bend over the card doll and hold them in position. Let the children colour and decorate their chosen garment.

Let them stick a cardboard tube behind the doll to allow it to stand up. Display the dolls dressed in their chosen outfits.

Questions
Which clothes do you enjoy wearing? Are they warm or cool? Which doll is going out? Going to bed? Going for a swim?

My shoes

Objective
To develop an awareness of different types of footwear for various people, activities and weather conditions.

What you need
A collection of different types of clean shoes (such as slippers, dancing shoes, wellingtons, football boots, baby boots), old catalogues, mounting paper, scissors, adhesive.

What to do
Put the shoes into a large box and mix them up well. Let the children sort the shoes into pairs. Discuss the various types of shoes. Who would wear them? What would they wear them for? Would they have been old or young, big or small? Ask the children to arrange the shoes in groups in order of size. Give the children catalogues and ask them to find shoes to cut out and mount on to paper, sorting them into different sets.

Follow-up
• Use some of the shoes to make footprints with a print tray. Cut a piece of foam rubber to fit a tray approximately 25 × 15cm. Soak the rubber with paint — black is particularly effective. Let the children make a footprint by holding a shoe and pressing it down into the paint then on to the paper.
• Encourage the children to observe footprints on wet and muddy days.

Questions
What are the shoes made from? Why are the slippers soft? How do they fasten? Which shoes do you like wearing?

Boys or girls?

Objective

To develop observation of peers, encouraging self-awareness and helping to establish a place within a group, and to develop the skills of sorting, counting and comparison.

What you need

Drawing paper, a large sheet of card, crayons, pens, chalks etc.

What to do

Ask the children to draw pictures of themselves. As they do so, encourage discussion of clothing, features etc.

Divide the large piece of card in half. Mount the pictures on the card using one side for boys, the other for girls. Add names to the pictures if there is room.

Questions

How many girls are there? How many boys? Are there more boys than girls? Are there girls in your family? How many children are there altogether? Can you draw a picture of your family?

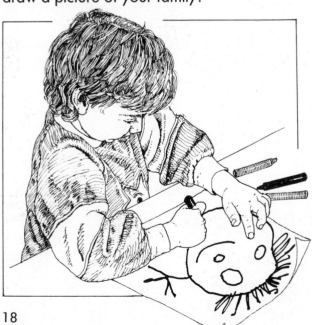

My family

Objective

To encourage children to think about and become aware of their place in the family.

What you need

Words of the rhyme 'How many people live in your house?', paper, pencils, crayons, felt-tipped pens, scissors, card, sugar paper, copies of photocopiable page 85.

What to do

Discuss families with the children — mothers, fathers, brothers, sisters, aunties, uncles — being sensitive to the fact that some children may not have a traditional nuclear family. Encourage free discussion and then let the children draw the members of their own family. Either frame the pictures with card or cut out the figures and mount them on to coloured sugar paper. Teach the children the song 'How many people live in your house?' (*Storytime*, BBC TV).

Using photocopiable page 85 as a template, let the children make card houses with opening windows and a set of family figures. Encourage the children to play freely with them, selecting mother, sister etc, according to the child's own family.

Questions
How old are your brothers and sisters? Who is the oldest member of the family? Who is the youngest? Who goes to work? Who cares for the baby?

Who helps me?

Objective
To promote an interest in the people whose work helps us and to increase the awareness of all the jobs they do.

What you need
Dust pan and brush, dusters, polish etc.

What to do
Introduce the children to the people who work in school – the caretaker, the cook, cleaner, secretary etc. Ask them to discuss their jobs with the children. Ask the children to decide on jobs that they could help with – perhaps collecting the morning milk cartons, sweeping up scraps of paper or sand, dusting and polishing furniture and tidying toys away.

Follow-up
Make a chart of jobs in the school, possibly using photographs of the people who help. Devise a list of jobs to share. This activity will involve daily discussion and promote an increasing interest and sense of responsibility towards the school environment.

Questions
Who looks after us at home? How could we help them? Who works in the village or town? What do they do?

Visitors' week

Objective
To broaden the children's experience of people who help them beyond their immediate environment.

What you need
People willing to come into school to talk to the children about their jobs, pictures, films and books about people who help us, pencils, paper.

What to do
Organise a week when it is possible to invite a different visitor into school each day to talk about their jobs. Discuss the plan with the children and make a list of the days, who is to visit and at what time. Let the children help write the invitations. After the children have listened to the visitor encourage them to ask questions.

Follow-up
Encourage the children to paint, draw or make models. Perhaps they could make a book, 'Mr Stevens is a policeman', for example, filling it with drawings, paintings, cut-outs from newspapers, photographs etc. Carefully discuss parents' jobs. Where do they work? What do they do? Remember that some parents may be out of work but will often use their skills at home. This discussion may reveal an untapped source of interest and provide you with enough prospective visitors to organise a second week!

Questions
Do all people work during the day? Which jobs have to be done during the night? Which jobs are done outside?

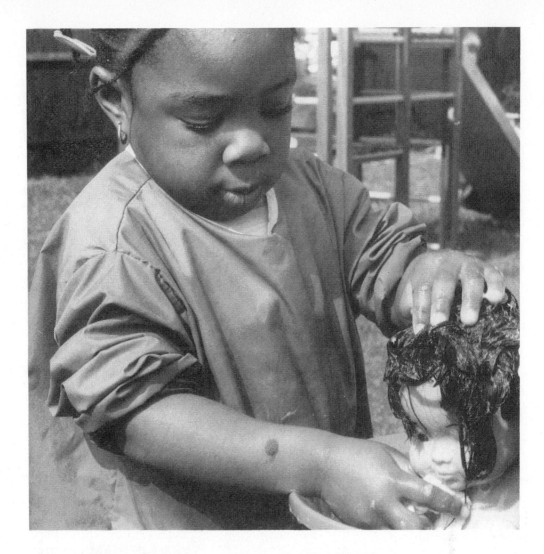

In and around the classroom

Chapter 2

The immediate environment of the classroom is a rich source of opportunities for investigation. Apart from the collections of natural materials, animals and plants that we can introduce into the room, the room itself and its contents can become a valuable study area. The water supply, lighting, heating, windows, furniture and so on, are all there to be investigated and provide good learning opportunities.

The children's own activities within an area should stimulate their natural interest and, as they ask questions or pass comments, the basic ideas and activities in this chapter can be used to their best purpose. Allowing the children to use the room themselves will encourage thinking and questioning, and provide them with plenty of first hand experiences which are so essential to the learning process. Organising furniture, helping to clear up, using the water, deciding when extra light or warmth is needed, will all help children to develop confidence in, and understanding of, their surroundings.

experience of the source of water may be limited to the above activity. However, further activities collecting rain, making rivers, and so on, will help develop an understanding of the original source of water and its value in our everyday lives.

Water – hot and cold

Objective
To investigate the water supply.

What you need
Two containers for each child.

What to do
Ask the children to fill their containers with water, one from the cold tap and one from the hot tap (making sure that the water is not too hot). Encourage them to feel the difference in temperatures and talk about the reasons for needing two taps. Help them to trace the source of the main water supply into school, noting where the pipes appear or disappear. Ask them to find the appliance that heats the water and, if possible, talk to the caretaker about the fuel it uses.

Follow-up
• Experiment with water play activities using warm and cold water.
• At this stage the children may not be able to visit a river or reservoir and their

Water play

Objective
To develop an awareness of the everyday uses of water.

What you need
A baby bath, old dolls, flannels, soap, a nailbrush, a washing-up bowl, plastic cups and plates, cutlery, saucepans, a cloth, dolls' clothes, soap flakes, buckets, sponges, mops, magazines, scissors, paper, pencils, adhesive.

What to do
Use the equipment to set up a variety of water activities for the children: bathing the dolls, washing dishes, washing clothes and cleaning up. Encourage the children to wash up the drinks cups and wipe the tables.

Ask the children to draw pictures or find pictures in magazines of water uses. Let them make a book with the pictures.

Questions
Can the children think of other uses for water? Do we need hot water?

Light sources

Objective
To encourage observation of the source of natural light.

What you need
A collection of large, strong cardboard boxes (preferably of equal size), adhesive, sheets of card or corrugated paper.

What to do
As a group activity, encourage the children to build the boxes into a house — big enough for two or three children to sit inside. Omit windows so that when a cardboard door is in place it will be almost dark inside. This should not scare the children as the door will be easy to open.

Ask the children to take turns to sit inside the house. Why is it so dark inside? Are our houses dark?

If you have an indoor play house, the same effect can be achieved by blacking out the windows with paper or dark curtains. You can also cover a climbing frame with dark material secured with safety pins.

Follow-up
- Help the children to create windows by removing boxes.
- Discuss the light inside the house.
- Encourage the children to draw pictures of houses. How many windows are there?

Questions
Where does the light come from? Why is it brighter at certain times of the day? Why does the light vary with different weather?

No electricity

Objective
To increase awareness of the use of electricity.

What you need
A darkened area (as in the previous activity), matches, jar, a night light, a torch or lantern, copies of photocopiable page 86, scissors, crayons, tissue paper, adhesive, string.

What to do
Show the children how various light sources operate and emphasise that they should always take great care with them. A night light in a large jar is the safest way of showing candlelight. Encourage the children to take turns to go into the dark area to experience the light made by any of the sources that you have. Some children may be afraid of the dark, so do not force them into the darkness. Carefully planned and supervised, this activity should create lasting memories and an appreciation of the use of electricity.

Ask the children to make a paper lantern using photocopiable page 86 and pieces of coloured tissue paper. Let them colour the lantern shape and stick scraps of tissue paper over the holes.

Follow-up

Read *Can't you sleep, Little Bear* by Martin Waddell.

Questions

How would we light our homes without electricity? Do you have a torch? What does it need to create the light?

Our furniture

Objective

To develop an awareness of the types and uses of furniture.

What you need

Large sheets of paper, felt-tipped pens, scrap materials.

What to do

Start by discussing with the children furniture in general. What is it? Why do we need it? Encourage the children to move around the room making a picture and number record of the furniture. Gather together and discuss the results.

Follow-up

● Invite the children to use waste materials, boxes, cards, cardboard rolls, paper scraps and so on to make model furniture, for example a chair for a doll or a bed for teddy.
● Tell the story of Goldilocks and the Three Bears and make chairs and beds in varying sizes.

Questions

What is our furniture made of? What furniture do you have at home? Which furniture do we use in the sitting room, the bedroom?

Our plants

Objective

To increase the understanding of the basic needs of plants.

What you need

Four flower pots each containing young seedlings, a large cardboard box, watering can.

What to do

Over a period of one week organise the children to water only one of the seedlings and keep it in the light. Keep another pot in the light, but do not water it. Cover the other two pots with a cardboard box to keep out the light and water only one of these. After one week ask the children to look carefully at the four plants.

Follow-up

Encourage the children to plant and grow a seed, pip or bulb of their own. Let them take responsibility for its care.

Bulbs can be planted in compost or leaf mould collected from a wood. Unless specially treated, bulbs can be simply planted in compost and watered lightly. Treated bulbs for early flowering should be planted, watered and stored in a cool, dark place until the flowers begin to form. At this point, bring them out into the light.

Questions

What do you notice about the plants? Which one looks the best? Why have the covered plants lost their colour? Why are some leaves drooping?

Our fish

Objective

To stimulate an interest in the characteristics and habitat of fish.

What you need

Books on caring for fish, a goldfish, a jar, a tank, gravel, water weed, fish food, clean pebbles, copies of photocopiable page 87, card, tissue paper, scissors, adhesive, pencils.

What to do

Explain to the children that they are going to have a goldfish as a classroom pet. Discuss what they will have to buy for the goldfish and what they will have to do to look after it. Read together books on how to care for fish.

With the children's help, cover the fish tank base with gravel and fill it with water. Let the water stand for a couple of days before introducing the fish into it so that any chlorine has time to evaporate. Carefully add water weed and a few pebbles.

If possible, organise a visit to a pet shop so that the children can help you choose their goldfish. Carefully carry it back to school in a jar. While it is still in the jar, encourage the children to observe it closely. Ask them to describe what they can see.

Gently introduce the fish to its new home, making sure that the water in the tank is roughly the same temperature as that in the jar.

Place the tank where the children can easily see it. Organise the children to take turns to feed the fish and clean out its tank.

Let the children make fish mobiles from card using the template on photocopiable page 87. Let them cut out fins and a tail from tissue paper and stick them on. Encourage them to base their fish as closely as possible upon their observations of the classroom goldfish.

Follow-up

• Ask the children to draw and write about their goldfish.
• Talk about other creatures that live under water.
• Visit an aquarium. Encourage the children to look closely at the colours and shapes of the tropical fish.
• Visit a garden pond to observe the fish.

Where shall we play?

Objective

To encourage the children to think about the use of play areas.

What you need

An outdoor play area, grass and asphalt surfaces, a set of balls.

What to do

Divide the children into two groups. Allow one group to play on the grass, the other to play on the hard surface. Encourage them to experiment with the balls; throwing, bouncing and rolling. After a while, gather the children together for a discussion on how they used their play area.

Follow-up

• Try this activity using bean bags — similar questions will arise.
• Talk about the best place for wheeled toys — do the children think it is a good idea to keep the climbing area separate?

• Encourage the children to think about and plan their play.

Questions

What were the children able to do with the balls on the hard surface? How did they use the soft grass surface? Were the activities different? Why? Did any of the balls get lost or go on a roof? Which area seemed to be the best for ball play?

Keeping tidy

Objective

To encourage positive thinking about waste.

What you need

A large, clear plastic bag.

What to do

Use the plastic bag to collect litter in the classroom for one whole day. Tie the top and keep the bag for the next day's activity.
    Encourage the children to inspect the contents of the bag through the plastic. What did we throw away? Could we have saved anything for re-use?

Follow-up

• Discuss materials that can be saved and used again and help the children to start collecting recyclable materials.
• Suggest craft activities using items that have been thrown away, for example, papier mâché, magazine scraps for scrapbooks, yoghurt pots for decorating and growing plants and so on.

Questions

Where does our rubbish go? Who collects it? Why must we never leave litter?

Mr Can

Objective

To encourage children (and parents) to collect aluminium cans for recycling.

What you need

A large, strong cardboard box which can be completely sealed, paint, collage materials, magnets, a large can, scissors.

What to do

Encourage the children to paint and decorate the box to make 'Mr Can' a collection box for aluminium cans. Help them to draw around a large can for his mouth and cut a hole this size. Set Mr Can in a prominent position in the classroom with the magnets close by. Explain to the children that if the magnets do not stick to a can, the can is made from aluminium and can be 'fed' to Mr Can. (Any steel cans can be taken to local steel recycling collection points.)

Encourage the children to 'feed' him whenever possible. When he is full, open him up, count the cans and pack them for a recycling collection. Discuss with the children the value and reuse of the material.

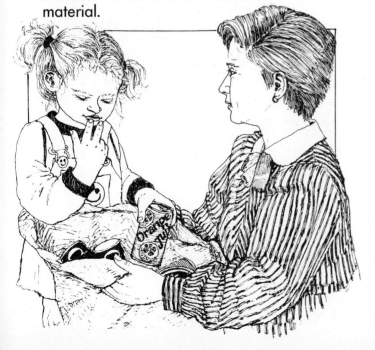

Questions

Are the magnets attracted to other objects? Do you know of any other materials which can be saved for reuse?

A tidy box

Objective

To encourage personal tidiness.

What you need

One cereal box per child, a hole punch, scissors, wallpaper, adhesive, paint, wool or string.

What to do

Cut the boxes and fold back the card as shown in Figure 1.

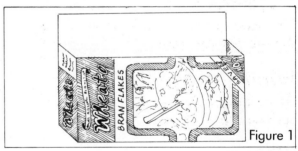

Figure 1

Ask the children to cover their box with wallpaper or paint. When the box is dry use the hole punch to make holes to hang the box. Encourage the children to use their box either to put their rubbish in or to store their pencils and paper.

Follow-up

• Invite the children to make a box for the classroom and discuss where it would be of most use.
• Let them make a box for a member of the family, not only for rubbish but perhaps for storing knitting, magazines or socks!

Questions

Is there always somewhere to put our rubbish? What should we do with it if there is no rubbish container? How do we store our possessions? Do we keep them tidy?

Collecting paper

Objective

To encourage an awareness of the many types of paper.

What you need

Paper, a pencil, paper-clips, crayons.

What to do

Help the children to make a list of items made from paper. The list could include items such as tissue paper, stamps, till receipts, cake cases and newspaper. Draw a simple outline of each item next to the appropriate word. This will help to encourage the children's interest in the written word and give them the opportunity to 'read' for themselves.

Give each child a piece of paper with the outline of the word 'paper' written on it. Ask them to colour in the letters. Write the child's name on the piece of paper and secure a paper-clip to the edge of each piece.

Ask the children to take their piece of paper home and to collect as many different paper items as they can, securing them to their piece of paper with the paper-clip. The collections which they bring to school will be very varied.

Follow-up

• Discuss the collections with the children. Count how many different types each child has collected.
• Let the children make a collage from their paper collection. Put the individual collages together to make a large mural.

Questions

Why should we recycle paper? What is paper made from?

Follow-up

● Help the children to make items out of paper, such as paper plate masks, flowers, fans, doilies and paper bag puppets.
● Read the *The Paper Puppy* by A. Broger and M. Sambin. Afterwards, help the children to draw, paint and cut out their own paper puppy. Talking about the puppy and recounting the story will provide a good opportunity to use memory and language skills.

Questions

What can't we use paper for? Why? Which jobs use a lot of paper?

Paper collage

Objective

To encourage an awareness of various textures of paper.

What you need

Different types of paper including sandpaper, shiny magazine paper, wallpaper, tissue paper, adhesive, frieze paper.

What to do

Collect a variety of paper of different textures, then help the children to make a paper collage.

Lay the frieze paper over a table and ask the children to stick on different samples of paper. Allow them to choose whether they are going to stick them on randomly or whether they want to group similarly textured paper samples together.

When the collage is finished, ask the children for their comments on how the different pieces of paper feel.

A paper book

Objective

To demonstrate the ways in which paper can be used.

What you need

Sugar paper or wallpaper, stapler, adhesive, various items made from paper, a pencil.

What to do

Make a large book from sheets of wallpaper or sugar paper stapled together in the middle.

On the first page write 'We use paper for . . .', then let the children stick the paper items on each page, according to their various uses. Add some simple explanatory notes on each page.

Even the youngest child will be able to help with the book and will be able to 'read' it. The book will be a valuable addition to the book corner.

Follow-up

Give the children a box of different types of scrap paper. Ask them to draw and cut out shapes from the paper. Let the children stick the shapes on to brightly coloured backing paper. Again, the shapes could be stuck on randomly or grouped together according to shape, colour or texture.

Questions

Which type of paper is rough? Which is smooth? Is any paper easier to stick than the others? Can you see through any of the paper?

Precious paper

Objective

To encourage an awareness of the value of paper and the importance of recycling.

What you need

Access to paper recycling bank, recycled paper products.

What to do

Talk to the children about what paper is made from and how it is made. Explain to them the importance of recycling paper. If you have a safe storage area, start a newspaper collection for recycling.

Take the children to deposit the newspapers in a paper recycling bank. Explain what happens to the paper and show them some recycled paper products.

Follow-up

● Ask the children to collect or paint pictures of trees to make a forest frieze.
● Using a saw, make some sawdust from a log. (Slightly rotting wood is easier to saw and makes good sawdust.)
● Rub some pieces of wood with sandpaper and let the children compare the textures.
● Teach the children the rhyme:
   If all the world were paper
   And all the sea were ink,
   If all the world were bread and cheese
   What would we have to drink?
                           (Traditional)

Questions

Why should we recycle paper? Whose families recycle paper? What other items can we recycle?

Our homes

Chapter three

Encouraging children to talk about their homes can give us an insight into their varied situations and experiences. We can draw upon this knowledge by introducing activities which will heighten their interest in their personal surroundings, thereby promoting a greater knowledge and understanding of their personal environment.

Home life and style will obviously vary greatly, even within a small group of children. For example, who lives in a house, a flat, a caravan? What are the main differences? This diversity can offer many good learning opportunities but with younger children, making use of common factors will be the best starting point; children will freely discuss and compare items that are familiar to them. For instance, wherever they may live and whatever their circumstances, they will have a door, windows and some furniture, so by using general features we can develop a common area for an investigation of 'homes'.

Our house

Objective
To increase an awareness of the use and contents of different rooms.

What you need
A large sheet of paper divided into 'rooms', old catalogues, paste, scissors, paper, crayons.

What to do
Decide with the children which 'room' is to be the kitchen, living room, bedroom, bathroom, and so on.

Encourage the children to choose and cut out pictures of furniture and other household items from old catalogues. Ask them to sort and stick them in the correct 'room'.

Follow-up
Using individual sheets of sugar paper, let the children draw, colour and cut out furniture or use a catalogue to make an individual 'room' picture to take home and discuss.

Questions
Why are most bedrooms upstairs? Where do we keep the car? What other rooms would we like to have in our house? Which room is the smallest? The biggest?

Which room?

Objective
To develop sorting, arranging and discrimination skills.

What you need
Two or three scraps of carpet, a cork tile or vinyl scraps, a selection of dolls' house furniture.

What to do
Arrange the carpet and tiles on either the floor or a table. Encourage the children to sort and arrange the dolls' furniture into 'rooms' using the different types of floor covering to represent the various rooms of a house.

Let the children feel and discuss the different types of flooring. Which one is soft, hard, smooth, patterned or plain? Can the children decide which is best for the kitchen? Why do they choose a soft one for the bedroom? Which is the smallest? Which is the largest?

Follow-up
- Investigate the flooring in school or at home.
- Make a table top 'feely' collage using as many different colours and types of flooring scraps as possible.

Questions
Why do we prefer carpet in the story corner? Why is there vinyl/tiling in the sand and water play area? Can the children remember the colour of their bedroom floor? Is it soft or hard, warm or cold? Which room do we sleep in, eat in, wash in?

Why windows?

Objective
To observe changes caused by window light.

What you need
A large cardboard box with a lid, a piece of carpet slightly smaller than the base of the box, card, small boxes, wallpaper scraps, adhesive, scissors, scrap materials.

What to do
Help the children to cut the wallpaper and stick it on to the walls of the box and put the carpet in the base. Use scrap materials to help the children make furniture or ask them to draw and cut out cardboard shapes to furnish the 'room'.

Help them to cut a small 'door' in the room which can be opened and closed. Replace the lid. Let the children take turns to peep into the room through the door. What can they see? How can they make the room light? Help them to cut windows in the box.

Follow-up
- Help the children to make a tiny 'room' inside a shoe box. Cut out the windows and cover them with clear or coloured acetate film. Make a 'peephole' to look inside. How different does the room look with coloured acetate film on the windows?
- Teach the children the song 'Who's that tapping on the window?' (*Oxford Primary Music – Stage 1*).

Questions
Can the children say if it is light or dark inside? How many windows did we need to cut in the large box? What would it be like if we had no windows?

My front door

Objective
To encourage observation.

What you need
An outdoor area.

What to do
Organise a walk and make children aware of all the doors you can see *en route*. Point out the differences – old, new, big, small, glass, wood, and so on. Notice the colour and adornments. Ask the children to check if their houses have a door-knocker or a letter box.

Follow-up
● Encourage the children to paint a picture of a door and add a descriptive sentence, for instance 'My front door is blue' or 'My front door has a brass letter box'.

● Give the children a piece of paper to take home, with the words 'My front door'. Encourage them to ask a parent or friend to help them to draw and colour their own door. When they bring the pictures back to school, discuss and compare them with the children. Mount them in a book or wall display.

Questions
Why do the children think they need a number on their house? Do they know their number, their address?

Locks and keys

Objective
To investigate locks and develop sorting, labelling, listening and discussion skills.

What you need
A box of assorted keys and locks, bolts mounted on smooth wood.

What to do
If possible, mount some of the locks and bolts on smooth wood to make them easier for the children to handle.

Encourage the children to play freely with the collection. The children will enjoy trying the keys and various bolts.

Follow-up
● Read *The Lighthouse Keeper's Catastrophe* by Ronda and David Armitage.
● Discuss the key collection with the children. Can they suggest where the various keys may have been used? Make labels for keys which fit obvious locks, such as on a car or front door.
● Make a collection of things which need keys.

Questions

How many keys do mummy/daddy use? Are they all for opening doors? What would happen if your front door key were mislaid?

A picture to make

Objective

To encourage observation.

What you need

A collection of old keys of various sizes, paint, toothbrushes, paper, an apron, paper towels.

What to do

Encourage the children to select some keys and arrange them on a sheet of paper, either in a random way or in a specific pattern.

Invite the children to press the toothbrushes into the paint and use their forefingers to flick paint over the keys and paper. When the paper and keys are well covered, let the children remove the keys carefully to reveal the 'picture'.

Ask the children to wash and dry the keys ready to use again.

Follow-up

● When the paintings are dry, encourage the children to try to match the keys to the pattern.
● Let the children experiment with other suitable objects or card shapes and make more spatter paintings.

Questions

Which type of key creates the best patterns? Can you achieve different patterns with the same keys lying on their other side?

My wallpaper

Objective

To increase the awareness of colour and pattern.

What you need

Paper, adhesive, a dolls' house, scraps of wallpaper.

What to do

Make an envelope for each child using the method described in 'Our photographs' on page 10.

Talk to the children about the walls in their homes. Ask them to describe them. Are they plain or patterned?

Investigate the interior of the dolls' house and compare the colours and textures of the walls in various rooms.

Ask the children to take the envelopes home to collect any scraps of leftover wallpaper their parents may have. Make sure the parents are aware of this request and emphasise that the children should not take any wallpaper off the walls! When the children return the envelopes, talk with them about the collection of colours, patterns and textures. Encourage the children to say which room the wallpaper was used in and who chose it.

Follow-up

Work together to make an interesting collage with the scraps or let the children stick their own pieces into a scrapbook. Add simple captions for them.

If some children have painted walls at home, encourage them to talk about the colours. Let the children mix paints to add a patch of colour to the collage or scrapbook.

In our shed

Objective

To develop the use of memory, observation skills and safety awareness.

What you need

Paper, old catalogues, scissors, crayons, adhesive, copies of photocopiable page 88.

What to do

Using photocopiable page 88, prepare shed models for the children and let them colour them in.

Give the children some old catalogues and ask them to find and cut out pictures of items that may be stored in a shed. Let them stick them inside the folded paper. Alternatively, the children could draw the contents inside the shed.

Ask the children to think about a shed, at their house or at a friend's or relation's house. Can they remember anything that is stored there? If possible, and under close supervision, take a group of children to investigate a shed.

Questions

Why do we store items out of the house? Why must we be very careful not to touch items in a shed? Do any living creatures hide in a shed? Do the children think the shed should be locked? Why?

Questions

If you have a garage at home, what do you keep in it? What other vehicles may we need to store? Did the garage smell? What did it smell of? Why must we be very careful with petrol and other similar substances that may be in the garage? Is it a good place to play? Why not?

Living in a flat

Objective

To observe a specific type of home and to develop understanding of mathematical concepts such as size, shape and numbers.

What you need

Building bricks, LEGO, mounting paper, felt-tipped pens or crayons, a visit to a block of flats, adhesive, paper.

What to do

Take a small group of children to visit someone living in a flat. Encourage them to look around and observe its features. Use both the staircase and the lift if possible. Back in the classroom, ask the children to try to build a block of flats with bricks or LEGO.

Ask the children to draw the rooms of a flat on separate sheets of paper. Mount them one above the other to create a block of flats. Encourage the children to add a lift or staircase, marking the different floors at the side.

Questions

How does a flat differ from a house? Would the children like to live in a flat? How many storeys are there in the children's collage? Would they use the lift or the staircase if they lived on the top floor?

The garage

Objective

To develop observation of size and shape and awareness of safety.

What you need

A garage to visit, toy cars of various sizes, bricks, LEGO or other construction toys.

What to do

Arrange a visit to someone's home to look at the garage and allow the children to look around inside under close supervision. What is stored in the garage? Ask the owner to talk about the use of the garage. How many cars will fill it? Is there enough room? How does the owner drive in and out? Talk to the children about the other items in the garage. Can the children see if the garage can be locked? How do the doors open and close? Back in the classroom, ask the children to use construction toys to build a garage for a toy car, making sure there is room to drive in and out. Can they make a garage big enough for two cars?

The building site

Objective
To develop an awareness of the way in which buildings are constructed.

What you need
Access to a local building project, a camera, a video recorder or a tape recorder.

What to do
Take the children to visit a building site and allow them to observe the work in progress from a safe distance. Help the children to take a few photographs, or let them video or tape record the site for a few minutes.

Back in the classroom, talk with the children about the building process, using the photographs and the recordings as a stimulus for discussion.

Play the tape and ask the children to try to identify the various sounds.

Repeat the activity at later dates to record the progress of the construction work.

Follow-up
• Help the children to mount their photographs on to individual pieces of card and use them for an ordering activity. Can the children recognise the progress of the building by looking at the photographs?
• Read *The Big Concrete Lorry* by Shirley Hughes.

Questions
What will the building be used for? What materials are being used? Which parts are wooden? Which parts are concrete? Which parts are brick? How many storeys will there be?

Looking at buildings

Objective
To encourage discussion and observation.

What you need
Paper, paints, a large wall area, blue or grey frieze paper, an outdoor area, junk materials, construction toys, adhesive.

What to do

Prepare the children by discussing buildings, perhaps during activities with LEGO or bricks.

Go for a walk, either within the school grounds or around the area, taking special notice of the buildings that can be seen. Encourage the children to look at their size, touch them and feel the texture. What are they built with? What are they used for? Point out the smaller buildings, such as sheds, garages, Portacabins and so on.

Back in the classroom, encourage the children to make a building of their own, either using junk materials, bricks or construction toys. Can they tell you what they have built, and what it is for?

Ask the children to paint pictures of the buildings. Help them to cut them out and mount them on frieze paper, grouping them to make an interesting display.

Follow-up

Use the 'Three Little Pigs' story to illustrate the strength of building materials.

Questions

Which building was the tallest? Which buildings were built with bricks, wood? What is your own house built with?

Where do we buy?

Objective

To encourage an awareness of different types of shops and commodities.

What you need

A classroom shop, empty packets and tins, vegetables such as carrots, onions and potatoes, dressing-up clothes, baby clothes, a mirror.

What to do

Help the children to organise a classroom shop. Encourage them to bring empty packets and tins from home to provide goods for a grocery or supermarket. Alternatively, use potatoes, onions, carrots and any other fruit or vegetables which do not bruise easily, to set up a greengrocery shop or stall. (After a few days, use the vegetables in a soup-making session.) Another idea would be to provide a collection of dressing-up clothes and baby clothes to make a dress shop. Provide a mirror and a private corner for changing.

Follow-up

Make a collection of pictures of objects which can be bought in shops. Magazine advertisements or old catalogues are a good source of pictures. Mount the pictures on to card, then help the children to arrange them in sets. Choose children to be shop-keepers. Allow the other children to take turns at being shoppers

and send them to the 'shops' with a shopping list. Do they know which shop to go to? Can they remember one, two, or three items? Check with the other children as they return with their pictures. Did they buy the correct items?

Questions
Where do we go to buy vegetables? Where do we buy bread? Where do we go for medicines?

Our pets

Objective
To develop an increasing awareness of the characteristics of pets and their different needs.

What you need
Paper, crayons, a large sheet of card, a camera or video recorder.

What to do
Talk to the children about their pets and, if possible, arrange for some to be brought into the classroom.

With the help of the children, plan a 'Pets' Morning' or 'Afternoon', when a parent or friend would be willing to bring a pet into school. Discuss with the children the times when the animals will arrive and depart and help them to compile a timetable, either by drawing pictures or writing the name of their pet.

Encourage the children to talk about the pets as they visit. Help them to question the adult looking after the animal. Take photographs, if possible, or make a video.

Follow-up
• Watch and talk about the video film with the children, or help the children to make an album of pets' photographs.
• Make a picture chart by asking the children to draw their particular pet and writing its name in bold letters. If the children do not have a pet, ask them to draw a picture of a pet they would like to have.

Questions
What differences did you notice between the animals? Which animals were able to walk to school? How did the others travel? Why do you think the goldfish travelled in his bowl of water?

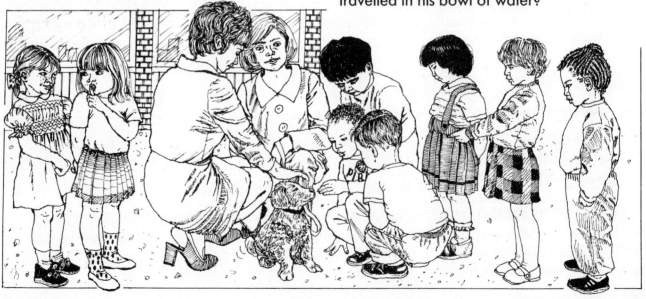

The weather

Chapter four

Every child will be familiar with weather changes and by encouraging discussion and observation we can increase their knowledge and create stimulating learning activities. The ideas in this chapter will help to consolidate the children's experiences and help them to build up an awareness of how things change, how living creatures adapt to varying conditions and how the children themselves alter their daily pattern and lifestyle as the seasons change. By using their own experiences, such as holidays and visits to relations in other countries, opportunities for discussing life in different climates may be introduced. Visitors to the classroom, relations, pictures and films can all help to broaden their understanding of the effects of the weather on everyday life.

Weather recording ✓

Objective

To encourage close observation of weather conditions and to introduce a simple form of recording.

What you need

Card, ruler, scissors, paper, pencils, felt-tipped pens, crayons, adhesive.

What to do

Use a ruler to divide up a piece of card, as in Figure 1. Explain to the children that the squares across represent the days of the week and the squares down represent the weeks of the month.

Today's **Weather** Month _____	☼ sun 🌬 wind ⁞⁞ rain ☁ cloud ❄ snow 🌫 fog
Monday	Tuesday	Wednesday	Thursday	Friday

Figure 1

Encourage the children to observe the weather conditions each day and draw an appropriate picture on a piece of paper to fit in the grid. Choose one of the pictures to stick over a square and allow the children to take the other pictures home — perhaps suggesting to them that they make a chart for their bedroom. Choose a picture from a different child each day so that no one will feel left out. As the chart fills, it will make an attractive wall display.

Follow-up

● Discuss the chart with the children at the end of each week — what does it tell them?
● Keep the chart and perhaps repeat the activity during another season. How does one chart compare with the other?

Questions

Which type of weather do you enjoy? Which pictures are the brightest and most colourful? What was the weather like yesterday? Last week?

✓ A rainy picture

Objective

To encourage an awareness of the distribution of rain.

What you need

Blue, green and grey frieze paper, copies of photocopiable page 89, paper, paints, felt-tipped pens, scissors, adhesive.

What to do

This activity is best undertaken on a rainy day.

Make a background for a frieze using the blue, green and grey paper to represent sea, grass and sky.

Use the template on photocopiable page 89 to make some cardboard shapes for the children and ask them to draw round and cut out their own umbrella shapes. Let them colour in the umbrellas using felt-tipped pens or paint. If they have their own umbrellas, suggest that they colour their cut-outs to match.

Let the children look out of the window at the rain falling. Talk about the colours of the rainy sky. Look at the clouds and then ask the children to try to mix paint in the appropriate colours, before painting clouds on to the sky area of the frieze.

Ask the class to paint pictures of trees and ships. When the pictures are dry, let the children cut them out and stick them on to the frieze.

Let the children finish off their rainy day frieze by sticking on their umbrella pictures, then adding thin streaks of paint to represent rain.

Follow-up
- Let small groups of children go out into the playground with umbrellas. What can they hear? Does the wind move the umbrella about?
- Teach the children the rhyme 'The rain is raining all around' by Robert Louis Stevenson from *A Child's Garden of Verses* .

Questions
What colour or pattern is your umbrella? Why do umbrellas need to fold up? What happens to the rain that falls on the fields? What happens to the rain that falls on the sea?

Fun with raindrops

Objective
To observe the rate and patterns of raindrops.

What you need
Paper, pencils, paint, powder paint, kitchen roll, a shallow baking tray, teaspoons.

What to do
Let the children take their piece of paper out into the rain for a few seconds. Back indoors, ask the children to use a pencil

to draw around the wet spots. Let them use paint to spot the paper inside the pencil circles.

Let the children line a baking tray with some kitchen roll. Using teaspoons, ask them to put tiny amounts of powder paint on the paper. Take the tray outside and place it where the children can see it. Let the children watch the raindrops wet the paint and soak the paint into the paper. Encourage them to watch how the colours blend together.

Follow-up
- Let the children make a print from the raindrop pattern by pressing a sheet of paper into the wet paint.

Questions
What happens when raindrops fall on an umbrella? Where do the raindrops go that fall on the grass?

43

Making a spectrum

Objective

To observe the colours of the spectrum and experience the effect of the sun on water droplets.

What you need

A length of hose-pipe, a water supply, swimsuits, copies of photocopiable page 90, pictures or photographs of rainbows, felt-tipped pens.

What to do

When the occasion arises, take the children outside to look at a rainbow. Talk about the colours, the sun and the rain.

On a sunny day, show the children how to use a hose-pipe to make their own rainbow. Run the water through the pipe and partly cover the end so that the water jets out in a fine spray. Spray the water into the sunlight to create the colours of the rainbow. The children will always remember this experiment if you allow them to play under the spray afterwards, wearing their swimsuits.

Give each child a copy of the rainbow worksheet on page 90. Encourage the children to colour in the rainbow using the colours in the correct order. Let them have pictures or photographs of a rainbow for reference.

Follow-up

● Using a picture or a photograph of a rainbow for reference, let the children experiment and try to mix the colours with paints. They may need your suggestions and supervision for this. When the paints are mixed, encourage them to paint their own rainbow.
● Make a collage picture of a rainbow using scraps of tissue paper. Sorting the scraps and working together to paste the pieces in the correct colour order will lead to much discussion and promote co-operative work.

Questions

What did we need to make the rainbow? How many colours did you see? What are your favourite colours? Which colours of paint do you need to mix to make green or orange?

Matching colours

Objective
To recognise colours and experience taking turns.

What you need
A card 18cm square and clearly marked into six squares for each child, crayons of six rainbow colours (red, orange, yellow, green, blue, violet), small squares of card to cover the base cards, a small wooden brick, a yoghurt pot or similar container, scrap paper, adhesive.

What to do
Ask the children to colour the squares of their base card in the six colours of the rainbow. Help them to make a colour dice by colouring six small squares to fit the six faces of the brick and sticking them on. Let each child colour six small cards to match the squares on their base card. Mix up the card squares and put them in the middle of the table. Encourage the children to take turns to shake the dice out of the pot and cover with a card square the appropriate colour on their base card. The first to cover all of their squares is the winner.

Follow-up
Talk about other dice games – can the children devise another version of the colour game, maybe using scrap pictures or numbers?

Questions
Do you remember the names of the rainbow colours? Where else might you see these colours?

Fly a kite

Objective
To experience the movement of the wind.

What you need
Drawing paper, thin string or wool, sticky tape, adhesive, tissue paper scraps, crayons, photocopiable page 91.

What to do
Prepare a few card templates for the children using page 91. Ask the children to draw around the template, cut it out and colour the shape. Then add a length of wool for a tail securing it with sticky tape. Show the children how to twist a scrap of tissue paper and attach it to the tail with a spot of adhesive. Encourage the children to make and stick on several of these twists to the tails of their kites.

Follow-up
● Take the kites out into the wind and let the children run freely.
● Try using different types of paper for the kites.

Questions
What else can you see moving in the wind?

The wind blew

Objective

To increase the children's awareness of the wind and its strength.

What you need

A windy day, paper, paints, pencils.

What to do

Take the children for a walk on a windy day. Encourage them to look for the effects of the wind. Can they see anything that is blowing away? Release a paper bag or scrap of paper. Encourage the children to watch where it goes — can they catch it? (If they can't, make sure that you do and emphasise the fact that they should never leave litter.)

Follow-up

● Read *The Wind Blew* by Pat Hutchins. Ask the children to choose one of the items that blew away and paint a picture of it. Help the children to cut out the pictures carefully and mount them on a 'sky' background. Now ask them to draw around their hands and forearms (they may need some help with this), colour and cut them out. Let the children arrange these along the bottom of the background paper to represent people stretching to reach the items blowing about.

● Play a game. Collect the items mentioned in the story or pictures of the same. Arrange them in a group and cover them with a cloth. How many of the objects can the children remember? Take one away — can they guess which is missing?

● Encourage the children to colour a picture of the items mentioned in the story and cut out the items to make their own game to take home. Let them make a simple envelope to keep them in.

Questions

How can we stop things blowing away? Have you seen litter blowing about? What should we do with our own unwanted cartons and bags?

Drying the washing

Objective

Maths   *science*

To observe the drying properties of the wind and to develop sorting, ordering and matching skills.

What you need

Small items of clothes to wash, washing powder, a water tray filled with warm water, a washing line, pegs, a cardboard box, adhesive, scraps of paper, crayons, a length of string, sticky tape, paint.

What to do

Invite the children to wash the clothes in the water tray. Help them to rinse the clothes and peg them on to the line.

While it is drying, help the children to make a model clothes line by cutting out one side of the box. Ask the children to paint or line the box with paper to make a green base and blue sky. Make a hole on each side wall of the box for the children to thread the washing line through; secure it with sticky tape. Help the children to cut out clothes shapes using folded paper. Let them colour the shapes and hang them over the line.

Follow-up

● Using folded card, make a variety of cards for the children to practise sequence patterns, colour matching, counting and ordering skills. Hang a length of string across the room and ask the children to place the cards over the string in the correct order.
● Give the children a box of winter and summer clothes and ask them to sort them and hang them on a washing line.
● Read *Mrs Mopple's Washing Line* by A. Hewett.

Questions

How long does it take for the washing to dry? Which clothes dry quickly? Which clothes take longer?

Hot bricks

Objective

To experience the heat transfer from the sun.

What you need

Two house bricks, a sunny day.

What to do

Encourage the children to feel the bricks. Place one of them in direct sunlight and leave the other either in the shade or indoors. Leave them for several hours. Ask the children to compare the bricks — can they guess which brick was in the sun just by looking at it? What do the bricks feel like? How long does the brick which was in the sunlight stay warm?

Follow-up

● Repeat the activity using other substances such as wood, metal and plastic. Do these stay hot as long as the brick?
● Encourage the children to touch different items on a sunny day to feel the heat from the sun.

Questions

What happens when the sun shines on our ice creams? Do they stay the same shape?

Using the sun

Objective
To heat water using the sun.

What you need
A length of hose-pipe (preferably transparent plastic), two buckets, a water supply.

What to do
Draw water from the cold tap into a bucket and let the children feel it. Leave the bucket indoors. Attach the hose to the cold tap and run the rest of the hose out into the sun. Plug the open end of the hose so that when it is full and the water turned off at the tap, the hose-pipe will stay full of water. Leave the hose in the sunlight for several hours, then run the water from it into the second bucket. Let the children feel the warmth of the water and compare it with the bucket drawn from the tap indoors.

Follow-up
Experiment with shallow, transparent bowls standing on foil sheets. Explain in very simple terms how solar power is used to heat water.

Questions
Where does the water in the tap come from? How do we get warm tap water? What are hose-pipes used for?

Why does it melt?

Objective
To experience the melting effect of the sun's warmth.

What you need
Bars of solid chocolate marked into squares, paper cake cases, a large tray, a sunny day, access to a fridge.

What to do
Break the chocolate into squares, one for each child. Let the children feel how hard it is and ask them to place it in a cake case. Let them arrange the cases on a large tray and help to carry it out into the hot sunshine. Encourage the children to observe the chocolate as it melts.

Follow-up
Re-set the chocolate by putting the tray into the fridge. Check that the children are allowed to eat chocolate and if so, help them to ease it out of their paper case. Find another treat for any children who cannot eat chocolate.

Questions
What happened to the chocolate in the sun? Did it stay the same shape? What shape was it at the start?

Reflections

Objective

To encourage an awareness of reflections.

What you need

A window, several sheets of black paper or a black cloth, a black plastic bucket or similar dark coloured container filled with water, small mirrors.

What to do

Cover the inside of a window with black paper or fabric. Take the children outside and invite them to look into the window at their reflections. What else can they see reflected? Ask them to take turns to look into the bucket. Whose face can they see? Can they see the clouds above them? What happens if they ripple the water with their fingers? Give the children the mirrors and ask them to look at their reflection. How do they differ from the reflections they see in the window and in the bucket of water?

Follow-up

How many items can the children find in which they can see their reflections?

Questions

Where are mirrors used?

Let's look at shadows

Objective

To observe and investigate how shadows appear.

What you need

White chalk, card, pencils, scissors, cardboard rolls, adhesive, a large white sheet, a sunny day.

What to do

Encourage the children to observe their own shadow in the sunshine, standing still, moving or making statues. Ask them to look for other shadows.

Invite the children to draw and cut out a figure, an animal or a toy shape, and attach a cardboard roll to it to make it free-standing. Let the children take their finished shape out into the sunshine — they will make some interesting shadows. After experimenting with the shadows, ask the children to stand their shape in the sun and mark its shadow on the ground with chalk. Leave the shapes for an hour or so. Go outside again and look where the shadows are now. Can the

children say why the shadow has moved? Ask them to mark the new position — can they guess what will happen later in the day?

Follow-up

• Play a shadow game. Hang a white sheet outside so that the sun shines through it. Divide the children into two groups and let them take turns to walk behind the sheet while the other group tries to guess the identity of the shadows.
• Read *Bear Shadow* by Frank Asch and 'My Shadow' by Robert Louis Stevenson.

Questions

What happens when a cloud passes in front of the sun? Can you find any moving shadows? Can you find shadows that are still?

Autumn into winter

Objective

To observe changes as the weather becomes colder.

What you need

A large wall area, paper, paints, a camera, a deciduous tree.

What to do

Invite the children to choose a particular deciduous tree. Ask them to look at it closely sometime in late summer. Encourage them to notice the colour and amount of leaves — is the tree covered? Let them paint a picture of the tree, carefully matching the greens by collecting a few leaves and helping them to mix the paints. When the paintings are dry, cut the trees out and mount them in a group. Add the date of when the paintings were made.

After a few weeks, take the children to observe the same tree again and repeat the painting activity. Altogether, make about four paintings of the tree, finishing with the bare winter branches. Take a photograph of the tree at each stage and mount them on cards to make an ordering game for the children.

Follow-up

Repeat the activity in early spring as the leaves begin to develop and make another ordering game for the children.

Questions

Can you describe the different colours that you saw and painted? What colours did you need to mix as the tree changed? Were there more or less leaves as the winter approached? What will happen to the tree in the spring?

Clothes for cold days

Objective
To develop the concept of different materials and types of clothes for different weather.

What you need
A box of dolls' clothes, two dolls, scrap materials, paper, adhesive.

What to do
In small groups, help the children to sort the clothes into winter and summer piles. Ask them to dress one doll for a cold day's outing, the other for a warm sunny day. Talk about the outfits with the children. Which doll is wearing the most items of clothing? Can the children decide why this is? Do the textures of the clothes vary? Can the children say what materials they are made from?

Use the scrap material box and help the children to sort scraps and wool to make a winter and summer collage. Feel and discuss the materials with the children as they are used.

Follow-up
• Use the cardboard doll activity (see Chapter 1, page 16) for the children to make summer and winter clothes. Compare the two types with the children. The younger children may need some help with the outlining and cutting but the intervening conversation will be of great value, as will be the finished 'outfits'.
• Read *Thank you for a Woolly Jumper* by Patricia and Victor R. Smeltzer.

Questions
Which materials keep us warm, dry, cool?

Warm fingers

Objective
To encourage an awareness of keeping warm and to aid sorting.

What you need
A fairly large collection of old mittens and gloves, coloured paper, scissors, felt-tipped pens, balls of brightly coloured wool, adhesive stick, photocopiable page 92.

What to do
Encourage the children to talk about how they feel on very cold days and discuss how they keep their fingers warm. How many ways can the children think of? As a group activity, ask the children to sort the mittens and gloves into pairs. Ask them if they know which materials the gloves and mittens are made from.

Using photocopiable page 92, prepare a sorting activity by cutting out mitten paper shapes in four different colours. Ask the children to draw a 'washing line' across a piece of paper, sort out four pairs of mittens and stick them on to the picture in pairs.

Follow-up

Read *Five Little Foxes and the Snow* by Tony Johnson and Cyndy Szekere to the children, then let them use the mittens work sheet.

Questions

What colour are your gloves or mittens? Do they keep you warm and dry? What are they made from? What else can be made with knitting?

Detecting seasonal changes

Objective

To encourage an awareness of the changing seasons.

What you need

A scrapbook, paper, crayons, adhesive, a felt-tipped pen, a camera, an outside area.

What to do

Take older children for a walk around the school grounds, taking in as many natural features as possible. Do this, using the same route, either once a week or fortnightly. Encourage the children to observe the natural features that will be changing, the weather conditions and the clothes that they wear for their walk. Help the children to record their observations either in drawings or with a camera or simple notes written in bold print in a scrapbook. Add the current name of the month.

Follow-up

Use the scrapbook at story time to share with the children.

Questions

Is the weather getting warmer or colder? What changes do you notice in the trees? Why do we have to walk carefully when it is frosty?

All around us

Chapter five

This chapter is concerned with the investigation and study of
plants and creatures which are easily accessible to children.
Included are simple ways in which we can help children to
encourage more natural habitats to develop in their immediate
surroundings.

   The children will not have to wait for an organised trip to
explore and investigate. Discoveries can be noted at all times
of day and in all kinds of weather conditions.

By working on the activities in this chapter, children will learn to use their senses to gain knowledge of the living things around them which might otherwise pass unnoticed. Through this increased awareness, we can help them to appreciate, care for and be concerned about other living things.

'If we give every opportunity for observation and at the same time encourage the child's appreciation and reverence for wild life, we shall have achieved much,' *Activity Methods for Children Under Eight*, 1956 (Morrison and Gibb Ltd).

Looking at the sky

Objective
To encourage observation and discussion.

What you need
Individual gym mats or a groundsheet.

What to do
Take a walk with the children into the school grounds or nearby park or hillside. Find a suitable spot and ask the children to lie down (making sure that they are not looking into the sun). Encourage them to look at the sky – can they describe what they can see?

Follow-up
Ask the children to paint pictures of the sky. Repeat the outing in different weather conditions – a windy, stormy sky is particularly interesting to watch.

Questions
What colour is the sky today? Are there any clouds? Are they white or grey, large or small? Can you see anything flying in the air? Are there any birds or aeroplanes?

I can see space!

Objective
To develop observation, language skills and links with home.

What you need
Cardboard rolls (preferably from kitchen rolls), sugar paper, a collection of collage materials, scraps of coloured paper, adhesive, binoculars or a telescope.

What to do
Encourage the children to take turns to look through the telescope or binoculars. What can they see? Use the cardboard rolls to make their own telescope. Let them cover the rolls with bright paper patterns. Allow them to play freely with

the telescopes and suggest that they may like to look into space when the sky is dark. Let them take the telescopes home and discuss their observations the next day. (A clear day when darkness falls early and the moon is full is most suitable for this activity.)

Follow-up

• Provide collage materials for the children to make their own pictures of the night sky – ready-made silver stars are exciting for young children and a card template will help with cutting out the moon.
• Read *I Want To See The Moon* by Louis Baum or *Whatever Next!* by Jill Murphy.
• You could extend the activities into a space project.

Questions

What can we see in the sky at night? Can we see colours? What do we use to help us see when it is dark?

A 'leave alone' area

Objective

To closely observe plants and small creatures.

What you need

A safely enclosed outdoor area within easy reach of the classroom that can be allowed to naturalise, logs, shrubs, young trees.

What to do

Introduce the children to the person who is responsible for the chosen area and discuss the features of the area. The children may be able to help to clear any rubbish and prepare the area for

naturalising. Help the children to plant shrubs and young trees. Arrange for some tree trunks and logs to be moved on to the area. Encourage the children to search for seed pods from wild flowers to help the area to become established. Impress upon the children the dangers of eating wild seeds and berries. Dandelion and willow herb produce seeds prolifically. The children will enjoy releasing them into the wind or scattering them over the area. In areas where natural wildflowers are less abundant, commercial wildflower seed mixture could be substituted.

Follow-up

• Let the children visit the 'wild' area in groups of two or three, encouraging them to move quietly and carefully as the plants and insects begin to develop.
• Encourage the children to observe the area closely and help them to make a

chart or written record, noting the season and weather conditions with each recording.
• Pretend to be butterflies or snails or caterpillars.

Questions

Why is it important to allow wildflowers to flourish? What happens to the seeds that the flowers produce? How many different creatures have you found? Do the creatures move in different ways?

The log pile

Objective

To develop a habitat for insects.

What you need

A small undisturbed area, logs, soil.

What to do

Encourage the children to help to pile the logs, shaking soil between them. Make sure that the finished pile is stable. Leave the pile alone for as long as possible. (It is a good idea to embark on this project before a lengthy holiday period.) After several weeks, encourage the children to investigate some of the logs, taking care not to disturb the habitat too much. There should be a good selection of bugs to study. The children can either study them on the spot using magnifying glasses and mini microscopes or you can help them to carry a log carefully indoors, resting it in a shallow cardboard box. Replace the log and its inhabitants as soon as investigations are completed.

Follow-up

• Use books and, if possible, a video film to help the children find out more about the lives of the creatures they are studying. This is a good opportunity to emphasise the use of the insects and to encourage the children to develop a respect for small creatures.
• Further investigations at different times of the year will yield other creatures and you may be lucky enough for a hedgehog to take up residence if the log pile is big enough.

Questions

Why do the creatures like to live in and under the logs? How do the insects behave when they are disturbed? How many different creatures have you seen?

Follow-up

● Help the children to study any living creatures they may find with a magnifying glass or mini microscope.
● Encourage the children to draw or paint pictures of their finds. Compiling a book or chart would be a useful activity.
● Collect soil from different places and the results of this activity could be very different. Soil from a building site may yield very little, whereas garden or woodland soil may reveal a wealth of creatures, seeds, snails' shells, leaves and so on. If you have access to a sandy seashore, damp sand may also be interesting to investigate.

Questions

How are the creatures adapted to live under the ground? What do they eat? Where do the seeds come from? Which creatures discard their shells?

Investigating soil

Objective

To encourage observation and investigation skills.

What you need

A small patch where soil can be dug and collected, trowels, small containers, a bucket, old spoons or twigs, cardboard box, a bin liner, a magnifying glass.

What to do

Encourage the children to dig the soil and fill the bucket. Let them take the soil back to the classroom. Help them to line a shallow cardboard box with plastic. Tip the earth into it and invite the children to investigate it by moving it gently with the spoons or twigs.

Sand trays

Objective

To provide an opportunity for children to handle natural objects, and to encourage pattern making, counting, ordering and sorting.

What you need

Several old trays of different shapes, sand, a collection of shells, stones, twigs, nuts, conkers, acorns, old spoons, water, old magazines.

What to do

Help the children to dampen the sand. Encourage them to fill the trays with the sand, smoothing it over to make a level surface. The children can then use the collection of stones etc to make patterns in the tray, pressing them and gently into the sand. After each pattern has been completed, encourage the children to sort the objects into separate piles and smooth the sand ready to start again. After plenty of free play and experimenting with this activity, encourage the children to make simple sequencing patterns or pictures.

Follow-up
● Ask the children to look for patterns – perhaps in magazine pictures, on the floor, in brick walls and so on.
● A collection of patterns made from rubbings or freehand drawings would make an interesting wall display.

Questions
Where have the various objects come from? Were they found in the woods, the sea or the garden? Which are smooth, rough, round? How many of each have you used for your pictures?

Who lives in the water?

Objective
To encourage observation, language and creative skills.

What you need
Collage materials, wall space, paints, scissors, adhesive.

What to do
Organise an outing to a park, stream, lake or seaside; even a garden pond will increase their experience and enrich their language. Talk about the expedition with the children and let them choose a bird

or fish that they have seen to draw and cut out or make with collage materials. Put the individual pictures together to make a large wall display. Encourage the children to hunt through the collage collection and use a variety of materials for their pictures. Ask for their advice in arranging their creatures on the wall frieze – either above or under the water.

Follow-up
● Teach the children to sing 'There's a little white duck'.
● Visit a garden centre which sells fish for aquariums or ponds.

Questions
What helps the fish to move? How do ducks' feet differ from our feet? What other creatures live in the water?

As the nest is dismantled, carefully sort out the various parts for the children to see and feel. It may consist of feathers, hair, leaves, twigs and moss or scraps of man-made materials. Mount some of each on the card for the children to see how many different objects the bird collected and used.

Follow-up
● Collect pictures of other birds' nests, illustrating the use of different materials.
● Talk about different types of homes and the materials they are built with.

Questions
What are our houses built with? Where do the bricks, wood, tiles and so on come from?

Investigating a nest

Objective
To observe and understand birds' needs for natural materials.

What you need
An old bird's nest that has been used or abandoned the previous nesting season, card, adhesive tape, a large tray, pictures of birds' nests.

What to do
Place the bird's nest on a large tray and talk about it with the children. Can the children describe its shape? How big do they think the bird must have been? How would the eggs stay dry and warm? After a general discussion, help the children to take the nest apart carefully, explaining that the bird has finished with it and that they should always leave nests undisturbed, just in case they are still in use.

Our butterfly patch

Objective
To attract butterflies and to observe them closely.

What you need
An area similar to the 'Leave Alone' area (see page 55), seed heads of flowers, shrubs, photocopiable page 93.

What to do
On a summer's day, take a group of children for a walk and ask them to look out for butterflies. Encourage them to notice which flowers the butterflies favour and help the children to make a note of them, perhaps by drawing and colouring simple pictures.

Back at school, explain to the children that you are going to set up an area to attract butterflies. Try to collect and encourage the children to contribute seed heads and pods of the plants which the local butterflies frequent. The butterflies will need suitable food and plants for both adults and caterpillars. Plants such as buddleia, Michaelmas daisy, marigold, honesty and scabious are all nectar-bearing flowers and are relatively easy to grow. Wild nettles will encourage butterflies to lay eggs and moths will find dock, willow herb and privet useful food plants. A hawthorn or privet hedge will encourage both butterfly and moth caterpillars.

Follow-up

• When the area is established, encourage the children to look closely at the hedging and other plants to find eggs and caterpillars. Let them observe, using magnifying glasses *in situ*, whenever possible.
• Ask the children to watch for butterflies and make notes of the colours. These can later be identified in reference books.
• Give each child a copy of page 93 and ask them to arrange the pictures in the correct order to illustrate the life cycle of the butterfly.
• Use the observation of contrasting movements of the butterfly in a dance session. Several children can join up to become a many-footed caterpillar, while others can move lightly with butterfly wings.
• Read *The Very Hungry Caterpillar* by Eric Carle.

Questions

How do people change as they grow? Do they change their form as butterflies do? How can we help more butterflies to breed?

Spider webs

Objective
To encourage a positive attitude towards spiders and encourage observation.

What you need
A sunny autumn morning when plenty of spider webs are visible, photocopiable page 94, pencils, magnifying glasses, scissors, adhesive.

What to do
Take the children outside to look and wonder at the spider webs. Encourage them to look closely to see where a web was started and how it was joined to leaves and branches. Watch the spiders if possible and use magnifying glasses to see more details.

Give the children a copy of page 94 and let the children make their own web pattern. Encourage them to draw their own spider and cut it out to stick on to the web pattern.

Follow-up
● Find a broken spider web and let the children feel how sticky it is.
● Read *The Very Busy Spider* by Eric Carle.

Questions
Why has the spider built its web in a particular place? What does the spider do with its prey?

Looking at symmetry

Objective
To encourage careful observation.

What you need
Mirror tiles, wooden blocks, strong adhesive, paint, paper, a collection of symmetrical natural objects (for example, leaves, feathers, shells), butterfly pictures mounted on card and cut into halves, pressed leaves and ferns mounted and halved in the same way.

What to do
Prepare mirror tiles for the children. Mount the tiles on wooden blocks so that they will stand freely. Give the children the natural objects to investigate. Encourage them to observe the symmetry of the patterns. Let them experiment with the half pictures of butterflies, leaves and ferns, laying them next to the mirror to apparently create a whole object.

Using the paints, show the children how to make a symmetrical pattern. Fold a sheet of paper in half, open it up and drop blots of colour on one side. Fold the paper in half, and gently rub the surface. Unfold the paper to reveal the pattern. Encourage the children to experiment, perhaps cutting some of the pictures in half to place by the mirror.

Looking at trees

Objective
To observe the animal life that trees support.

What you need
Any tree or trees, old wallpaper books, card, adhesive, clear sticky-backed plastic.

What to do
Encourage the children to observe the tree or trees carefully. Help them to collect sample leaves or fruits for study indoors, but warn them not to put any of the plant parts into their mouths. Ask the children to note any birds or animals that use the trees. Talk about the differences between the trees and compare leaves.

Help the children to press some leaves (an old wallpaper book or a pile of newspapers is useful for this). When the leaves are dry, help the children to mount them on card and cover them with sticky-backed clear film. (This will prevent them drying out and help to keep them flat.)

Encourage the children to draw or paint any creature they have seen using the tree. Collect the pictures together and ask the children to stick them in a scrapbook. Alternatively, you could make a large tree shape to put on a wall and add the creatures to it. Bark rubbings from the tree or trees will also add interest to the finished work.

Follow-up
Read *The Very Worried Sparrow* by Meryl Doney.

Questions
Why do the creatures live in the tree? Do you have a tree in your garden or know of a tree that bears fruit or berries? Who eats the fruit? Why must you be careful not to touch any fruit or berry without asking an adult first?

Blossom for the classroom

Objective
To observe and appreciate the fruitfulness of trees.

What you need
A collection of stems, either dried twigs or budding branches (pruning leftovers are useful), a large empty jar, newspaper, powder paste, paint, PVA adhesive, pink, white and green tissue paper, access to a tree or bush in 'blossom'.

What to do
Observe a blossom tree or brush with the children. In the classroom, discuss the colours and type of blossom with the children.

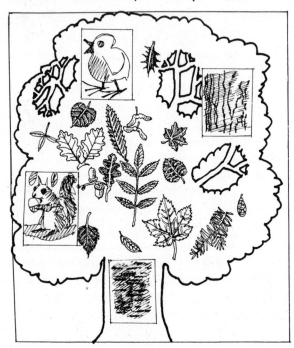

To make 'blossom', show the children how to cut or tear the tissue paper into small pieces, then scrunch each piece and, using a dab of strong adhesive, attach it to a twig. If there were leaves on the tree you looked at, the children can use the green tissue paper in the same way.

To make a vase, ask the children to tear the newspaper into small pieces and gradually cover the jar with several layers of it, sticking it with fairly wet powder paste. Encourage them to smooth the paper and leave the jar to dry. When the jar is dry the children can paint it and 'varnish' it with a coat of PVA adhesive (this dries like a clear varnish).

Ask the children to arrange the twigs in the jar to make an attractive decoration for the classroom.

Follow-up

Use books and films to help the children understand the development of fruits and berries on trees and bushes.

Questions

Which insects did you notice on the blossom tree? Can you find the place on an apple or orange where the blossom once grew? What other fruits do you know?

Raising plants

Objective

To encourage an appreciation of living plants and to develop a caring and responsible attitude towards plants.

What you need

Plant pots, small stones, compost, water, plant tops, seeds, plant cuttings, tree seeds, small bottles.

What to do

Encourage the children to grow plants from a variety of 'starting points' such as cuttings, seeds, bulbs or vegetable tops.

Save the tops of carrots, beetroots and parsnips (about 2cm of the vegetable should remain), and help the children to plant them in soilless compost with a layer of small stones or gravel in the bottom of the pot for added drainage, so that the trimmed leaf crowns show just above the surface. Ask the children to water them gently to keep the compost damp. The top will produce an attractive leafy display.

New plants can easily be grown from the runners of plants such as spider plants, mother of thousands and the common strawberry. Show the children how to push the baby plants into a pot of compost. When they have developed their own roots, snip them from the mother plant.

Ivy, busy lizzie and coleus, for instance grow easily from cuttings. Cut strong side shoots from the mother plant, just below a leaf joint. Let the children pot them in small bottles of water. When the roots have grown, the children can plant them in small pots of compost. Geranium cuttings can be put straight into compost.

Tree seeds need to lie dormant before they are ready to germinate. Ask the children to store their tree seeds until December when they can plant them in pots and put them outside until March. Protect the pots from birds and mice by covering them with a piece of fine wire mesh. In March, let the children bring the pots indoors to encourage the plants with some warmth.

Follow-up

● Sunflower seeds can be started off indoors. They are large enough for children to handle and germinate quite quickly. Their subsequent growth is rapid and impressive. When the plants are about 6cm high, let the children plant them outside. You don't even need a garden — they grow easily in a bucket in a sunny position.
● Help the children to collect the seeds from the mature sunflowers to plant the following year. Ask them to leave some for winter food for the birds.

Questions

Which types of plant are easy to grow? Which types of plant grow slowly? Do plants survive without water? Do plants grow in the dark?

Looking at flowers

Objective

To encourage an appreciation of the beauty of flowers.

What you need

Any fine example of a flower — perhaps two or three blooms, colouring paper, crayons, chalks or felt-tipped pens.

What to do

Display the chosen flowers on a low table where the children can observe them closely. Talk about the flowers and then encourage the children to see if they can find in the room any small objects of a similar colour. Help the children to arrange the objects around the flowers.

Prepare some colouring sheets for the children by drawing the chosen objects in simple outline and adding the name of the colour. Give each child a photocopied sheet and encourage them to find crayons, chalks or pens to match the objects and flowers to colour their sheets. This will involve a great deal of discussion, naming and comparing the objects and appreciating the flowers as the centre-piece.

Follow-up
• Ask the children to bring in a flower, either from their garden or from a plant or from a bunch of flowers at home. They could use this as the basis for another colouring activity.
• Take the children for a quiet walk, looking at and discussing any flower you may find along the way.

Questions
Do you know the names of the flowers? Which is your favourite colour?

Collecting seeds

Objective
To discover different types of seeds.

What you need
A collection of small plastic containers (empty film spool cases are ideal), small dishes (either lids from jars or party dishes), magnifying glasses, a mini microscope.

What to do
During early autumn, when many plants are fruiting and making seeds, talk to the children and show them one or two examples of seeds. Encourage them to put forward their own ideas of which plants have seeds and give them a small container to take on a seed hunt, either in the school area or at home where they can ask the help of an adult. Always warn the children of the dangers of eating unknown wild plant material. Display the resulting collection in the dishes. You could also show some of the plants that the seeds came from. Let the children look closely at the seeds through the magnifying glasses and miscroscope. Point out the differences in the seeds.

Follow-up
• Read *The Tiny Seed* by Eric Carle.
• Let the children plant some seeds in small containers. Put gravel or small stones in the bottom of the containers before adding a layer of compost. Grass, candytuft and mustard and cress seeds are all suitable for growing indoors and will germinate quickly.

Questions
Can you count the seeds from a pod? Can you count the seeds from a poppy head? Why do you need a magnifying glass to look at some of the seeds? What will grow from the various types of seeds you have collected?

A spring display

Objective

To encourage an appreciation of the natural beauty of flowers.

What you need

A fairly large quantity of daffodil or crocus bulbs, a shallow tray, a bulb planter, two jam jars containing water, a selected, undisturbed grassy area.

What to do

In early autumn, buy a large bag of bulbs. Tip the bag out onto a shallow tray. Let the children look at, handle and talk about the bulbs. Ask each child to select two or three. Move out to the appointed area of grass and ask the children to spread out so that they are well spaced, and gently toss their bulbs onto the ground around them. Help them to pop the bulbs into holes just where they land using the bulb planter — this way the flowers will bloom in an attractive random array.

Save one or two bulbs for the children to grow indoors using a jar of water so that they can watch the roots and shoots develop. Choose a good-sized bulb or a jar with a narrow neck. Rest the bulb on the neck of the jar so that the water is just touching the base of the bulb.

Follow-up

Set up other types of bulb to grow indoors or in tubs outside so that the children can compare their growth rate, flower formation, colour and so on.

Questions

Why didn't the bulbs grow in the bag? What do the bulbs need to help them grow?

How many potatoes?

Objective

To give firsthand experience of growing food.

What you need

A potato for each child (these need not be 'seed' potatoes but seed potatoes do give better results), lolly sticks, string, a dibber, a patch of ground, one or two strong adults, an oven, scrubbing brush.

What to do

Choose the right time of year for planting potatoes to do this activity. Let the children handle and talk about the potatoes, and talk about planting them in soil. Invite the children to help the adults prepare the soil — maybe two or three children at a time. It will be a valuable and enjoyable experience for them. When the soil is ready, help the children mark out planting lines using string and

sticks. Let each child plant his own potato making a hole with a dibber and marking it with a labelled lolly stick.

When the potatoes have grown, the children can each dig up their own collection, carefully putting them in bags or buckets. Encourage the children to count how many have grown from the original potato that was planted. Help them count the total number produced.

Let the children wash and scrub the potatoes and suggest that they bake them in an oven. Eaten warm with a little butter or grated cheese, they make a delicious snack.

If there is little available space to grow potatoes, several potatoes can be grown in a black plastic bag filled with good, damp compost. The potatoes can be pushed either into the top of the bag or into holes made in the sides.

Follow-up

• Make an interesting wall chart by asking the children to draw, colour and cut out a picture of their original potato. Mount them with the children's names. When the real potatoes are harvested, the children can draw and cut out pictures of their own number of potatoes to add to the chart.
• Help the children to grow a tomato plant in compost or a grow-bag. Emphasise the importance of regular watering. Provide a cane to support the plant as it grows. Show the children how to prick out the tiny side shoots as they appear. Feed the plant if the compost is not particularly rich. Let the children spray the plant with water to encourage the fruit to set, or they could brush the flowers with a little cotton wool.

Questions

What other vegetables grow under the ground? As well as baking the potatoes, how else can they be cooked?

Favourite fruits

Objective

To encourage visual and tactile observation.

What you need

A selection of five or six fruits, paper, crayons, pencils, a knife, a large dish.

What to do

Display the fruits and let the children gently handle and talk freely about them. Encourage them to feel and smell each fruit. How do they differ? Can the children say which are hard, soft, round, long? Encourage the children to try to draw the fruits, discussing the shapes and colours with them.

Follow-up

• Help the children to peel and cut up the fruit and arrange it on a dish.

- Let the children choose and taste pieces of the fruits. Be aware of possible food allergies among the children.
- Invite the children to plant some fruit pips. Give them each a jam jar and ask them to put some small stones in the base, followed by a 2—3cm layer of soilless compost. Help the children to press their pips in the top of the compost, water them gently with warm water and cover the top of the jar with polythene secured by an elastic band. Stand the jar in a warm place, perhaps by a radiator, as the seeds need to germinate. This will take two to eight weeks. When the seed has formed a tiny plant, help to pot it in a flower pot.
- The children could also plant fruit stones from fully ripe fruit. Carefully crack the hard shells with nutcrackers, squeezing just enough to fracture the

shell. This will speed up germination. It is best to do this activity in late winter or spring.

Questions

Which fruits taste sweet? Which taste sour? Which fruit has a crisp texture? Which is soft? Which is your favourite fruit? Which other foods are made using fruit? Which fruits come from warmer countries?

Guessing the fruit

Objective

To encourage language skills.

What you need

A collection of familiar fruits or vegetables, a shallow cardboard box.

What to do

Look at and discuss the fruit or vegetables with the children. Stand the cardboard box on its side on the table. Put the fruit into the box. Let the children take turns to stand behind the box, choose a fruit and try to describe it to the other children. Can the children guess which fruit is being described? Younger children may need a little help but with practice they will begin to think and talk about colour, shape and smell.

Follow-up

Add one or two less familiar items of fruit (for example, kiwi fruit). The children will enjoy learning new names and tasting the fruit when the game is finished.

Questions

What other tastes do you enjoy? Which vegetables grow under the ground?

A woolly jumper

Objective
To help understand another source of natural materials.

What you need
Ideally, a visit to a sheep farm or pictures of sheep, a video film or books about sheep, photocopiable page 95, crayons, scissors.

What to do
Talk with the children about sheep and their woolly coats. If at all possible, take them to a sheep farm. Let the children collect scraps of wool to take back to the classroom and display it.

Give each child a copy of page 95 and ask them to colour the pictures, then cut them into individual squares. Can the children arrange the pictures in the correct order to show the story of the woolly jumper?

Follow-up
• Read *Thank You for a Woolly Jumper* by Patricia and Victor Smeltzer.
• Encourage the children to make a collection of items made with wool.
• Read *Mr Nick's Knitting* by Margaret Wild.
• Invite someone into school to demonstrate knitting skills.

Questions
Have you got any garments that have been made with wool? Are woolly clothes warm or cool to wear? What do woollen clothes feel like? What colour is wool before it is dyed?

Classroom chicks

Objective
To give firsthand experience of eggs hatching.

What you need
An incubator (these can often be borrowed from a field centre or, information about it from a science centre), ten fertile eggs (arrange to buy these from a farm, but check with the farm that they would like the young chicks after a couple of months), an enclosed run and box for the chicks, paper, scissors, Blu-Tack, crayons.

What to do
Set up the incubator and mark all the eggs with a cross. While the eggs are incubating, allow the children to take turns to turn them gently over each day. When the chicks hatch keep them under a brood lamp. It is possible to look after them for up to eight weeks, providing you have the facilities.

If it is possible to borrow a broody hen instead of an incubator, this would be better still. In this case, you would need a small hen house and run for the hen and chicks plus some food for the hen.

Follow-up

● Encourage the children to draw and paint pictures of the eggs and chicks.
● Help the children to make a plan of the incubator. Arrange the pictures of eggs on the plan using Blu-Tack so that as the chicks hatch, the egg can be replaced by a picture of a yellow chick.
● Visit the farm at a later date to see the chicks and note how they have changed.

Questions

How do wild birds incubate their eggs? Who turns them over?

Hickety pickety

Objective

To encourage observation, counting and memory skills.

What you need

Sugar paper, paper, crayons, scraps of straw, collage materials, a box of ready-cut paper 'eggs'.

What to do

Following a visit to see some hens, teach the children the traditional rhyme:
    Hickety Pickety my black hen
    She lays eggs for gentlemen.
    Sometimes nine and sometimes ten,
    Hickety Pickety my black hen.

Figure 1

Make a hen template, using Figure 1 for reference. Encourage the children to make a collage picture of a hen by drawing around the template, colouring it black and cutting it out. Mount the hen on sugar paper and add collage materials for food and straw. Let them add nine or ten eggs.

Follow-up

Enjoy another rhyme together such as Chook, Chook, Chook, Chook (from 1, 2, 3, 4 by Mary Grice, this time using felt cut-outs on a flannel graph. The children will enjoy reciting the rhyme and counting the chickens.

Questions

Do any of you have hens at home? Who enjoys an egg for breakfast?

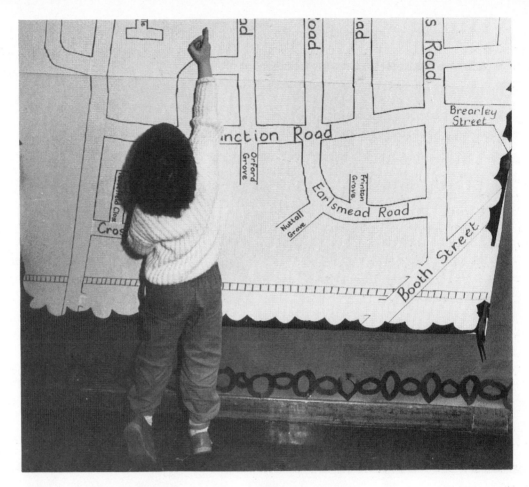

Travelling about

Chapter six

The activities in this chapter will help to awaken children's interest in the way in which roads, railways and rivers are used. Not all schools are within easy reach of railways and rivers, but perhaps you could take the children on an outing to such a location. On your return to school, you can discuss with the children what you have seen and develop their interest with the activities given here and the use of books and videos. Any expedition, however simple, must, of course, be well supervised and special care should be taken near roads, railways and rivers. Careful planning and safe vantage points will result in happy outings and successful investigations.

Making a roadway

Objectives

To encourage discussion and increase knowledge of road use, pencil and scissor skills.

What you need

Large sheets of paper cut into lengths, a black felt-tipped pen, scissors, lolly sticks, card, Plasticine, a pencil, card, a selection of small vehicles, Highway Code.

What to do

Prepare each sheet of paper for the children by drawing with a black felt-tipped pen a road approximately 12cm wide. Make light pencil markings down the centre of the road. Encourage the children to cut carefully along the black lines, then using the black pen draw carefully over the centre lines. The roads are then ready for play and can either be used individually or joined together and stuck to the floor to make a more complex layout. Joining the roads together will encourage co-operative and constructive play.

Corners and roundabouts can be added and by using a Highway Code book, the children can discuss road signs that may be appropriate. These can easily be made from lolly sticks, circles and triangles of card and Plasticine. The children will probably need help to draw the signs.

Questions

How do we cross the road? Where do we cross? Where do the cars have to stop? Why do drivers and pedestrians need signs and coloured light signals?

Before motor cars

Objective

To encourage a sense of history and to practise using a variety of information sources.

What you need

Books, old photographs.

What to do

Young children often have difficulty in appreciating a sense of the past so it is important to keep the work simple. Thoughts about the past and comparisons with the children's own lifestyle make a valuable starting point for later studies.

Through discussion in small groups, encourage the children to think about movement — how we travel from place to place and how goods are transported.

Do the children realise that in the past there were no cars or lorries? Can they think how things were moved without them? Where might they find out? Talk about people who remember a long time ago. Do they know any person who is old? Suggest that they look for books and pictures illustrating times past. Where would the children go to find books? Have the children seen television programmes about times past? How did the people travel?

Follow-up

• Help the children to discover books, pictures and so on related to the subject.
• Do the older members of their families have photographs of horses, carts, barges, steam trains and so on.

Questions

How do you travel to school? How long would it take to walk? How does daddy or mummy get to work? Could they get there without a car? How do you travel for your holidays?

Riding in the bus

Objective

To encourage co-operative work and observe the use of a bus.

What you need

First hand experience of a bus ride or observations of buses, large wall space, paper, crayons, scissors.

What to do

Following an outing on a bus or observations of buses, prepare a large cut out shape of a bus. Encourage the children to draw, colour and cut out a picture of themselves. Help them to mount the figures in the bus, gradually filling all the spaces as the pictures are completed. Let them complete the area around the bus with pictures of what they saw on the route — birds, cows, horses, houses and so on.

Follow-up

Let the children make their own bus using chairs or large bricks. Encourage them to play an imaginative game by providing a driver's hat, tickets, a bell and perhaps an old steering wheel.

Questions

How many people can travel on a bus? How many can travel in a car? How many cars would be needed to transport all the people in the bus?

A traffic light picture

Objective
To increase awareness of the use of traffic signals.

What you need
Thin card or good quality paper, red, orange and green paper (or crayons for colouring), adhesive, scissors, pencils.

What to do
Prepare the paper for the children by folding the sheets in half lengthways. Divide one half into three sections using pencil lines. Ask the children to cut along the lines to the fold, then cut out circles of coloured paper and stick them behind each flap in the right order.

Follow-up
• While they are making the picture, help the children to learn the names of the colours and the meaning of the signal.

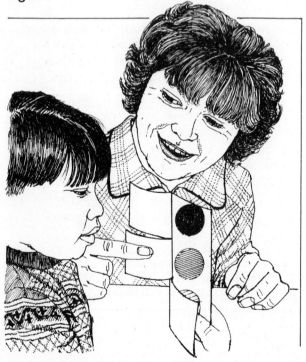

• Make another similar game using the signals on a pedestrian crossing.

Questions
What do the different lights mean? Can you think of any other places where lights are used to signal?

Holding hands

Objective
To remind children to hold an adult's hand when walking by or crossing the road.

What you need
Paper, pencils, crayons, scissors, adhesive, mounting paper.

What to do
Encourage the children to draw around one of their hands (they may need help with this). Then ask them to draw around your hand. Ask them to colour and cut out the shapes, then mount them on paper with the fingers together (as holding hands). Add a caption such as 'Hold Mummy's hand' (let the children choose who they would like in the caption).

Follow-up
Invite the children to take the picture home and ask an adult to put it up where the children can see it as they leave the house.

Questions
How do we keep our pet dogs safe when walking by the road? Do you hold hands with an adult when you are in a busy shop or market place?

A simple map

Objective
To experience using a very simple map.

What you need
A work bench or table covered in large sheets of white or light coloured paper.

What to do
Create a simple map by drawing roadways and adding symbols or shapes for houses, trees and so on. Ask the children to use their fingers to trace their way along the roads. Talk about the shapes explaining what they represent. Using a specific starting point, can the children find their way to the school? Or to the garage? Which way would they go to the park? Can they find their way back again?

Follow-up
- Make worksheets for the children to colour and trace with their fingers.
- Find an old road map book for them to look at and investigate.
- With groups of older children, much discussion should develop through observations related to their surroundings.

Making a route

Objective
To encourage thinking about direction and movement.

What you need
A large hall or clear outdoor space, exercise mats or carpet squares, planks, large wooden bricks or old tyres, a large gym mat or a carpet, paper, pencils, old rolls of wallpaper, Blu-Tack or sticky tape.

What to do
Set the children a task to make a route with the gym mats and other equipment from one point to another so that they can walk across without touching the floor. Arrange a large gym mat or piece of carpet to represent a river and encourage them to build a bridge with some of the equipment. Rivers and railways can also be made from old rolls of wallpaper which can easily be rolled up to use another time. They can be anchored to the floor with Blu-Tack or sticky tape.

Follow-up
Give the children a sheet of paper the same shape as the area they have been using. Can they draw the route and the river?

Using the river

Objective
To illustrate the use of boats for carrying goods.

What you need
First hand observation or a video film of boats using a river, milk cartons, general junk materials, scissors, a water tray or paddling pool, small bricks, acorns, nuts or conkers.

What to do
Take the children to a commercially-used waterway or show them a video of boats carrying goods. Encourage the children to use junk materials to make boats, freely experimenting with different types of boxes and cartons. Suggest making boats with the milk cartons. Help the children to cut around the carton to form a boat shape that will float very successfully.

Follow-up
Let the children load their boats with 'cargo' using small bricks, conkers, acorns or nuts.

Our journeys

Objective
To observe different forms of travel.

What you need
A large sheet of card, felt-tipped pens, vehicle templates, crayons, scissors, old magazines or travel brochures.

What to do
Discuss with the children the different journeys that they have made — a journey to school, to gran's or on holiday. Encourage them to draw around the appropriate template or draw freehand to illustrate the way in which they travelled. Assemble a chart for the children so that they can see how everyone made their journey.

Follow-up
Help the children to collect pictures from magazines and travel brochures to make a scrapbook or collage of ways to travel.

Questions
How do you travel to school? How does mummy or daddy travel to work? Why do we sometimes have to travel by air?

Expeditions

Chapter seven

The main emphasis of the activities in this book is on firsthand experience — investigating and discovering the child's immediate environment. Venturing further afield increases the opportunities for discovery and gives children an increasing self-confidence in and awareness of their environment. Making the most of local features and amenities leads to fascinating and rewarding investigations and the interest aroused can be channelled into a variety of follow-up activities. The suggestions in this chapter for expeditions may lead to further ideas for which the follow-up activities can be adapted.

Let's have a picnic

Objective
To organise and experience a planned expedition.

What you need
Cups, plates, food, drink, a blanket.

What to do
Let the children organise their own picnic. Encourage them to check how many items they will need for the number of children taking part. Help them to

prepare food and drink; they could make simple sandwiches and cakes. Discuss where the children are going to have the picnic. How are they going to get there? How will they carry the food? If they are planning to take dolls, how will they carry them? What will they need? Talk about the use of prams, trucks, bicycles, and so on. The children will obviously need you to accompany them but you should leave them to do their own organising as much as possible.

Follow-up
• Talk about other picnics the children have attended.
• Read *Bear's Water Picnic* by J. Yeoman and Q. Blake.
• Make a book of drawings and captions about the picnic.

Questions
What is the best weather for a picnic? Which is your favourite picnic food or drink? When is it best to take cold drinks? Hot drinks? What can we use to help to keep the drinks hot or cold?

A listening walk

Objective
To encourage listening and increase awareness of surroundings.

What you need
A notepad and pencil, a small tape recorder (if possible).

What to do
Organise small groups to take a walk, either inside or outside the classroom.
Set off and stop at regular intervals and encourage the children to listen. Write down the children's suggestions of

things they can hear. Tape record any significant sounds, if possible. Repeat the activity on another occasion using another route. Perhaps choose different weather conditions for an outdoor expedition.

Follow-up
• Discuss the list with the children and compare notes on sounds — were they loud or soft? Pleasant or unpleasant?
• Help the children make a chart or a book to record the sounds. With older children, add the date and weather conditions so that comparisons can be made on later walks. Use the tape recorder to remind the children of the sounds you heard.

Questions
Where did we hear the most sounds? Where was it quiet? Which sounds were loud? Do you prefer natural sounds to mechanical sounds, such as . . .?

The post office

Objective
To investigate a feature of the local environment.

What you need
Paper, envelopes, adhesive, 'stamps', 'parcels', balance scales, toy money, a telephone, cardboard, cardboard rolls, sticky tape, crayons, pencils, brown parcel paper, a large cardboard box, adhesive labels, rubber picture stamps, empty tins and boxes, thin card, red paint, paper fasteners.

What to do
Ask the children to bring to school a letter or postcard that they have received. Talk to the children about them. How did they arrive? Where did they come from? Do the children know what they need to send something through the post? Ask the children if they know where there is a post-box. Using the cardboard rolls and card, let the children make models of a post-box.

Encourage older children to either write a short letter or make a card to send through the post. Help the children to wrap and address a parcel ready for posting. Compare the size and weight of the parcel with the letters. Which do the children think will cost the most to send? Organise a visit to a post office to buy stamps and post the letters and the parcel. If possible, arrange for the children to see the letters being collected or sorted during the visit.

Follow-up
• Make a pretend post office in the classroom and let the children take turns to work behind the counter. Use a large cardboard box for a classroom post-box

and encourage the children to write short letters using folded scrap paper for envelopes. Make 'stamps' for the children by using sheets of small adhesive labels and rubber picture stamps. Wrap tins and boxes for the children to post as 'parcels' – the counter assistant will enjoy weighing and pricing them. Taking turns at delivering the post is another enjoyable activity – receiving post is also fun at the end of the day.

• Make model post-boxes with the children. You will need to prepare the card for the children by cutting circles slightly larger than the diameter of the rolls. Show the children how to cut to the centre of one circle. They should then slightly overlap the card and glue the edges to make a top for the post-box.

Ask the children to stick the top and the base to the roll, paint it red and cut a slit for the letters. (You may need to help them with this.) Using an adhesive label or a piece of paper encourage the children to write collection times for the front of their post-box. By cutting a 'door' in the box, the children will be able to use the model for posting small notes and pictures. Use a paper fastener to secure the door.

Questions

Do you know your address? What else can we buy at the post office? Do you know what time the post is collected from the box nearest your home? If not, can you find out? Can you describe how to get to your nearest post-box?

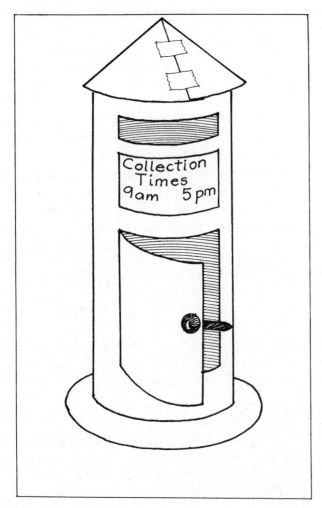

Visiting the elderly

Objective

To encourage an awareness of other people in the community.

What you need

A residential home for elderly people within easy distance, paper, pencils, pictures of elderly people, a small gift.

What to do

While discussing age, talk to the children about elderly people. Do they know anyone who is very old? How do they know they are old? Where do they live? How do they move? Show the children pictures of older people – what do they notice? Explain to the children how people find it more difficult to move as they become older and that if they have no family, they need to live in a special place where they can be looked after.

Do the children think that the older people would like them to visit and perhaps take a small gift? Help the children to write a letter to a local home asking if they may visit. Let the children make something to take with them for the people in the home — either a picture, a decoration or a gift. There are lots of ideas in *Bright Ideas for Early Years: Christmas Activities* (Scholastic).

On the day, tell the children to move and talk quietly in the home. Encourage them to ask questions about the people's families. Perhaps they could look at family photographs or mementos. Ask the residents if they would like the children to sing them some songs. A piano is usually available; if not, take a tape recorder to sing along to.

Follow-up
The children could send a present or cards at Christmas and keep in contact with the home. Perhaps you could make a termly visit.

Questions
Did you like the home? Did you notice flowers, pictures and so on? What sort of chairs did the elderly people use? Did some of them need special chairs? Did the people move slowly or quickly? Did they need help to move?

The bakery

Objective
To investigate the source of a loaf of bread.

What you need
A small local bakery, wheat or corn grains, a plant pot, compost.

What to do
Arrange to take the children to the bakery when the baker has time to show them the bread making process. Encourage the children to look at the flour and the machinery, and watch the baker making the dough. Show the children the grains of corn that are grown to make the flour. Look at the other products in the bakery and buy a few samples to cut up and taste back in the classroom.

Follow-up
• If you have the facilities, it is fun to make bread rolls in the classroom — handling the dough, baking it and tasting it is a valuable activity. You can use any simple bread recipe and fresh yeast is available from bakeries or some supermarkets. If not, dried yeast can be substituted.
• Let the children plant some corn or wheat in a plant pot. It will grow rapidly.
• Tell the story of *The Little Red Hen* to the children.
• Act out the story of *The Little Red Hen* or make cardboard puppets with the children to tell the tale.

Questions
What else did the baker sell besides bread? Which of the products were sweet? Which were savoury? Why are some of the loaves cut into slices?

Pick your own

Objective
To give firsthand experience of gathering fruit or vegetables.

What you need
A fruit or vegetable farm within easy reach, a small container for each child, one or two baskets, a basic picnic (if time and facilities allow).

What to do
Visit the farm to check that they are prepared to accept a group of children and find out which fruit and vegetables are ready for picking. Talk to the children about the visit — emphasise the need to move carefully amongst the plants. Explain to them what the ripe fruits will look like and how to pick them. Tell the children that they may fill their own container which will eventually be tipped into the larger baskets.

At the farm, walk with the children, pointing out the different types of fruit and vegetables that are growing. Help the children to pick, weigh and pay for the produce. If you have time, gather together for a picnic before returning to school.

Follow-up
• Select a bowl of fruit for the children to try, or vegetables to cook.
• Help the children to weigh or count the produce into equal quantities and stick a price label on them. The children will enjoy selling to their parents at home time and the recouped money may be used to finance any transport you had to use or go towards another outing.
• Making a mixed fruit and vegetable stall can be fun. At the fruit farm, divide the children into groups with one adult to each group. Direct them to different areas, each group picking one particular type of fruit or vegetable. Back in the classroom, arrange the produce to make a 'stall' and sell as suggested.

Questions
How many different fruits and vegetables did the farm grow? Which ones grew above the ground? Which ones grew below the ground?

Faces, see page 11

What do we wear? see page 16

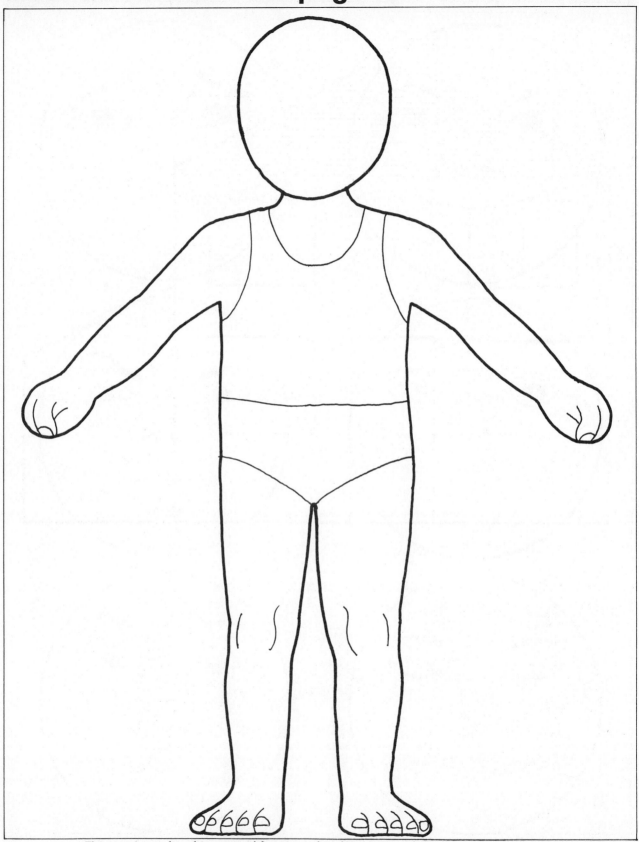

My family, see page 18

No electricity, see page 23

Our fish, see page 25

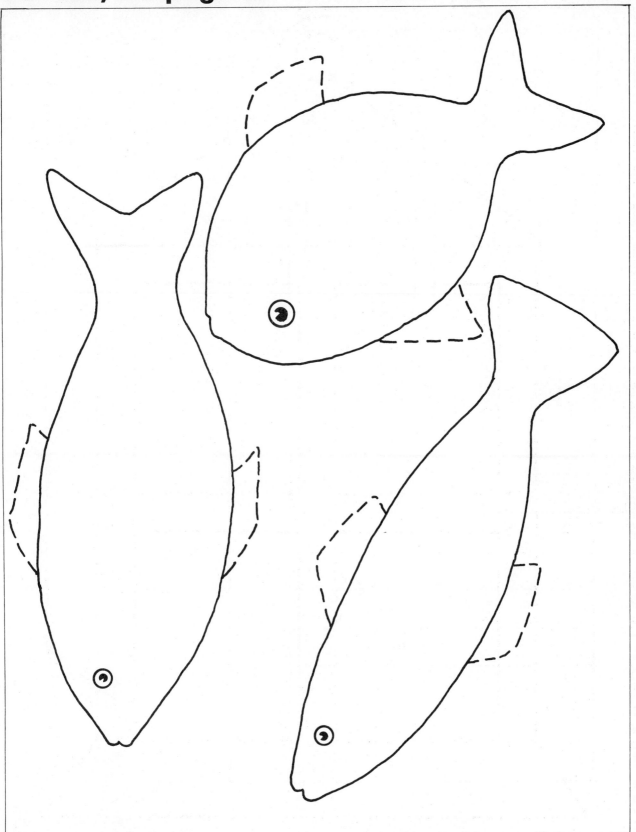

In our shed, see page 36

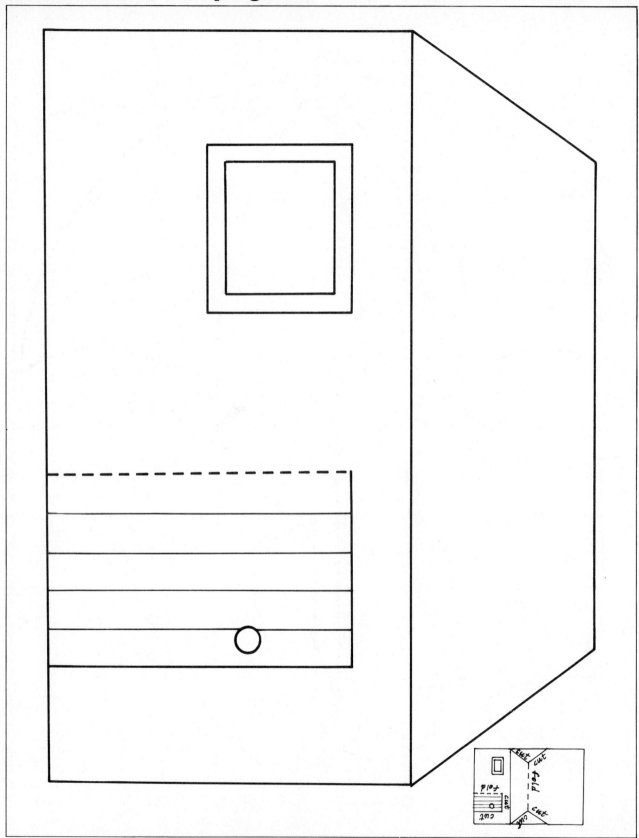

Rainy picture, see page 42

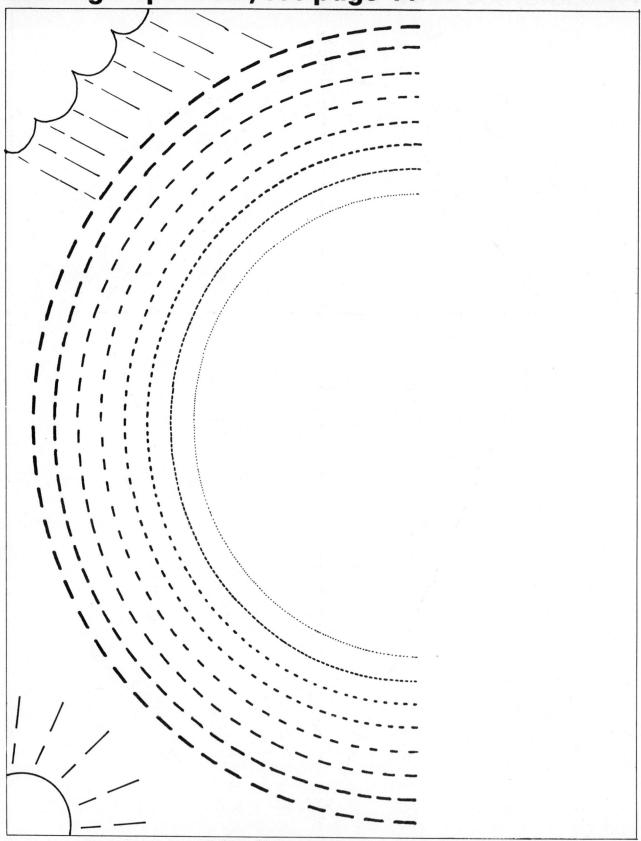

Fly a kite, see page 45

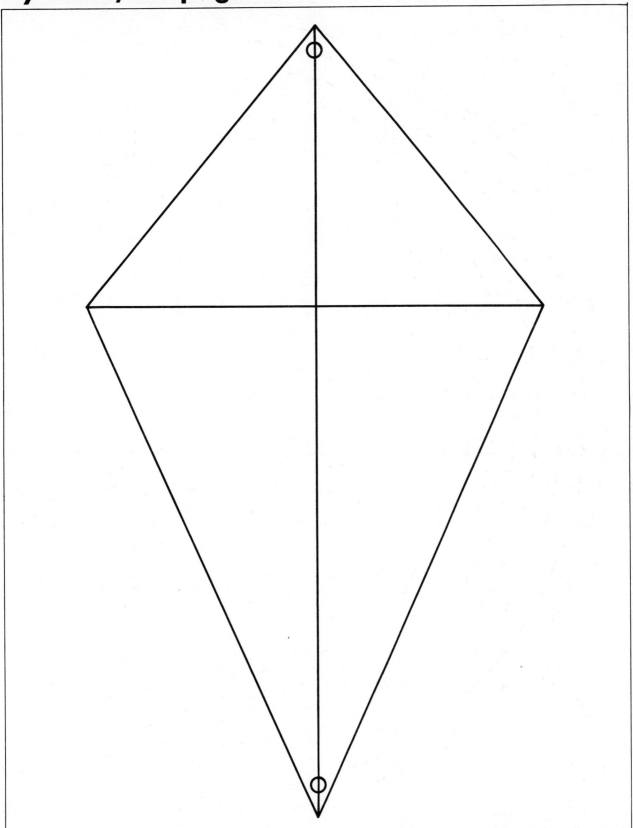

Warm fingers, see page 51

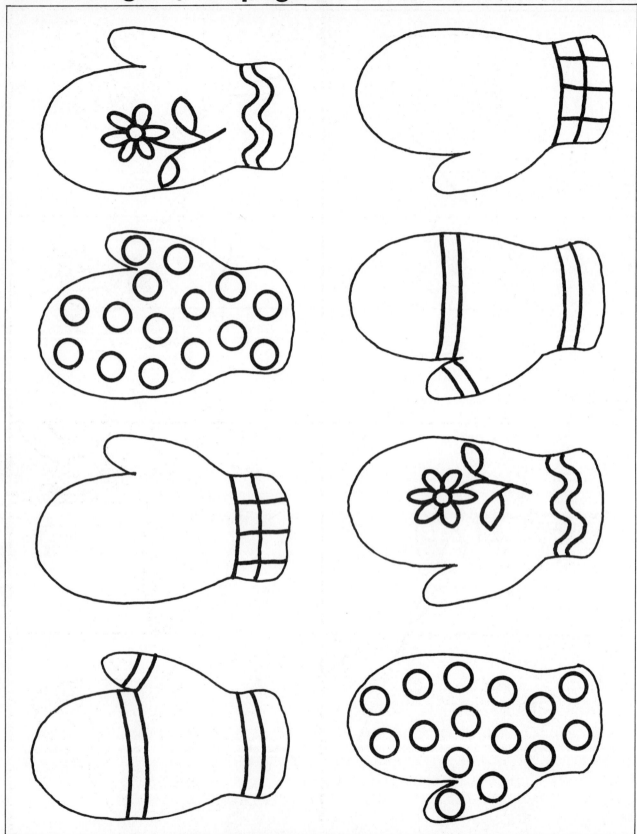

Our butterfly patch, see page 59

Spider webs, see page 61

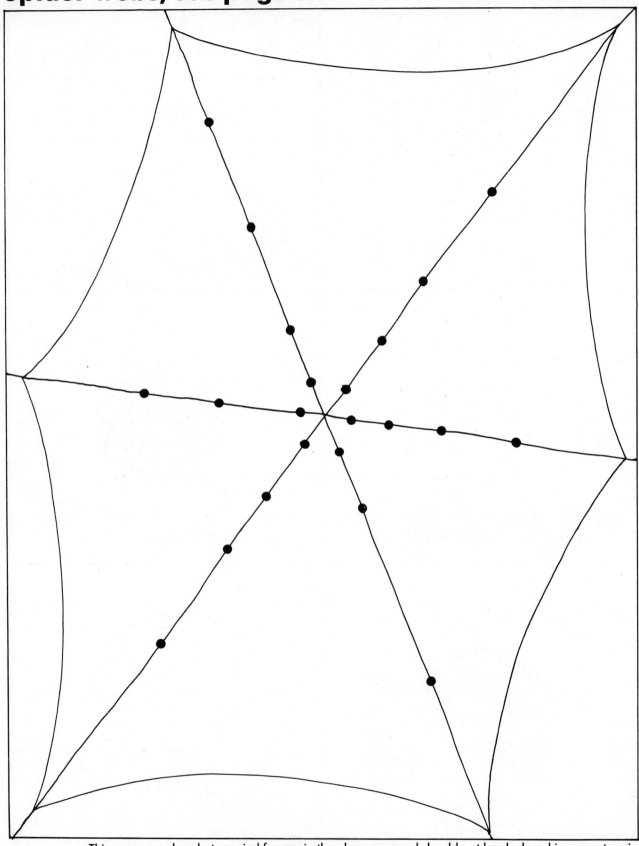

A woolly jumper, see page 69

Book list

A Child's Garden of Verses, Robert Louis Stevenson (1989) Gollancz.

Bear Shadow, Frank Asch (1989) Picture Corgi.

Bear's Water Picnic, J. Yeoman and Q. Blake (1986) Macmillan Children's Books.

Can't You Sleep, Little Bear? Martin Waddell (1990) Walker Books.

Five Little Foxes and the Snow, Tony Johnston and Cyndy Szekere (1979) World's Work.

I Want To See the Moon, Louis Baum (1985) Magnet Books.

Mr Nick's Knitting, Margaret Wild (1989) Hodder and Stoughton.

Mrs Mopple's Washing Line, A. Hewett (1970) Puffin Picture Books.

1, 2, 3, 4, Mary Grice (1972) Warne.

Oxford Primary Music – Stage 1, Leonora Davis and Jean Gilbert (1986) OUP.

Thank You for a Woolly Jumper, Patricia and Victor R. Smeltzer (1983) Lion Publishing.

The Big Concrete Lorry, Shirley Hughes (1991) Walker Books.

The Lighthouse Keeper's Catastrophe, Ronda and David Armitage (1988) Picture Puffin.

The Paper Puppy, A. Broger and M. Sambin.

The Tiny Seed, Eric Carle (1988) Knight Books.

The Very Busy Spider, Eric Carle (1988) Hamish Hamilton.

The Very Hungry Caterpillar, Eric Carle (1974) Picture Puffin.

The Very Worried Sparrow, Meryl Doney (1979) Lion Publishing.

The Wind Blew, Pat Hutchins (1978) Picture Puffin.

This Little Puffin: Finger Plays and Nursery Games, E. M. Matterson (Ed.) (1991) Puffin Books.

Whatever Next! Jill Murphy (1985) Macmillan's Children's Books.